Fox-Hunting

The Duke of Beaufort's Hounds

How they drive to the front! – how they
         bustle and spread,
Those badger-pied beauties that open the
         ball!
Ere we've gone for a mile, they are furlongs
         ahead,
As they pour like a torrent o'er upland and
         wall.
There is raking of rowell and shaking of
         rein
(Few hunters can live at the Badminton pace),
And the pride of the stable's extended in
         vain,
And the Blues and the Buffs are all over the
         place.

*A verse written for my father by
G. J. Whyte Melville after a good day
near Tetbury.*

Fox-Hunting

The Duke of Beaufort

DAVID & CHARLES
Newton Abbot   London   North Pomfret (Vt)

British Library Cataloguing in Publication Data

Beaufort, Henry Hugh Arthur FitzRoy Somerset,
   Duke of
   Fox-hunting.
   1. Fox-hunting
   I. Title
   799.2′59′74442   SK285

ISBN 0−7153−7896−1

First published 1980
Second impression 1980
Third impression 1981
Fourth impression 1983
Fifth impression 1985
Sixth impression 1987

Printed in Great Britain by
Redwood Burn Limited, Trowbridge, Wilts
for David & Charles Publishers plc
Brunel House Newton Abbot Devon

Published in the United States of America
by David & Charles Inc
North Pomfret Vermont 05053 USA

Contents

Acknowledgements

I want to thank Gloria Cottesloe who gave up so much of her time to this project, helping me in every possible way with the general style, writing and approach to the whole subject. Without her invaluable and professional help, the book could never have been published.

I should also like to say how grateful I am to my old friend Peter Farquhar for his advice and help. I am indebted to Brian Gupwell, my Huntsman, and to Brian Higham, my Stud-groom, for their co-operation; and to Mr Bywater, my secretary, for his help with the illustrations.

Although I no longer hunt my hounds, I still enjoy my hunting enormously
(Frank H. Meads)

*I started my riding days on a donkey. Here I am with my mother, my sisters,
Blanche and Diana, and the Stud-groom, Mr Dyer, 1904*

Soon I graduated to a pony

1
How My Fox-Hunting Life Began

Although I do not actually remember learning to ride I cannot truthfully say I remember a time when I could not. I began, as so many children, especially of my generation, always have done, on a donkey at the tender age of two years old. It was not long before I graduated to ponies, but as I was my father's only son, and he was fired I suppose by the ambition that I should swiftly take to the saddle, he tended to overmount me – in fact, so much so that at one time I was in serious danger of losing my nerve. I received no formal tuition at that stage, just being told by my mother's second horseman, Fred Matthews, who was with my family for fifty years and who was put in charge of me, to lean well back as I came to the jumps. In common with any other youngsters mounted on a pony that was pulling his arms out and which he really could not manage fortified only by such well-meant but misguided advice – naturally I fell off. Fortunately, however, like most small boys, I bounced, and was soon back in the saddle again and, what is more, I did not lose my nerve.

Then at last came one golden day in the Easter holidays when I had just arrived home from my private school. The train had been late and I had to hack out to try to find hounds, riding a new pony called Woodcock, a topping little animal and which must have been, I think, a twelfth-birthday present. Suddenly, on reaching the brow of a hill, I spotted a fox that had evidently done some work. Remembering my father's vehement injunctions to me in the hunting field, I stood like a rock, and also held my tongue. A moment or two later, to my thrilled excitement I heard hounds, and soon the leading hound was in sight followed closely by the pack, and behind them galloped the Huntsman, George Walters, who had not been

A proud moment as I rode off with my own pack of harriers – an eleventh-birthday present from my father

Drawing a field of roots

It was some years before I hunted my own bitch pack of hounds. I am riding the first horse I ever bought and one of the best I ever rode

long at Badminton. I found out later that the Field were far behind struggling in the Kilcot Hills, so George and I had a flying start alone together with the hounds.

I think George Walters must have realised how unsuccessful I had been in the field up to then, for as I galloped along by his side, probably holding on to the pony's head far too tightly, he called across to me: 'You'll be all right. Lean forward and leave him alone when you come to the jumps.' Never have truer or happier words been spoken, for as I relaxed and took George's advice, leaning forward at every fence, I felt the power of that wonderful pony as it responded to my every touch. That spring day I shared a wonderful hunt with the Huntsman, gaining more and more confidence with every minute. A spark was lit in me that soon grew into a flame destined to last the whole of my life – a true and dedicated love of fox-hunting in the deepest sense.

I cannot explain how I felt as I sped along, my riding improving at every fence, but I am sure that everyone else who has had the good fortune to feel the exhilaration, the excitement and what is more, the sense of achievement that is experienced when a successful hunt

Towards the end of his life my father was seldom far from the scene of action, sitting in his car accompanied by his dog wearing Beaufort colours

is concluded, will know what I mean. It is by no means altogether a feeling of personal achievement, but comes from a subtle combination of being at one with both horse and hounds. Hunting is so much a matter of teamwork, it is never a sport in which it is possible to single out a particular person for individual glory, for there are so many people behind the scenes responsible for setting the stage and providing the props that lead to a successful day.

In this book I am going to try to explain who they are, what their duties are and how, ideally, those duties should be carried out.

> *Not for lust of killing, not for the place of pride,*
> *Not for the hate of the hunted we English saddle and ride,*
> *But because in the gift of our fathers the blood in our veins*
>   *that flows,*
> *Must answer for ever and ever the challenge of 'Yonder he*
>   *goes!'*

Will Ogilvie

2

The Fox

Of all the wild animals in this country, to my mind the fox is quite the most game and certainly the most beautiful. I find it is almost impossible to pick up a book on fox-hunting without coming across the immortal words that R. S. Surtees gave to Jorrocks:

> . . . the 'oss and the 'ound were made for each other and natur' threw in the fox as a connecting link. His perfect symmetry and my affection for him is a perfect paradox. In the summer I loves him with all the hardour of affection; not an 'air of his beautiful 'ead would I 'urt; the sight of him is more glorious than the Lord Mayor's show, but when the autumn comes then dash my vig how I loves to pursue him to destruction.

Jorrocks was in fact voicing the feelings of the many generations of dedicated fox-hunters both before and after his time. Believe me when I say that a fox is safer in one of my coverts during the summer than anywhere else in the world!

First and foremost it must be remembered that the fox is essentially a nocturnal animal, lying low during the daylight hours, and only venturing forth with extreme caution at night to hunt. In the main foxes live in earths which they have either dug themselves or have taken over from other earth-dwelling animals, often sharing one with a badger. But in their desire for a dry bed foxes will sometimes climb trees and lie out on a fork or bough, and at Badminton they are often to be found in the trees around the park, and certain of these trees have always been sure finds.

Much depends on the weather, of course, for when it is very wet the fox is more apt to lie underground than outside in, for example, open hill country, where although the rocks and crags provide a shelter of sorts, they are not really sufficient to protect him from prolonged rainfall. He will choose a dry drain or a natural or artificial earth, whether they be in or out of covert.

Individual foxes vary in their ways and habits just like human beings. The ones that are really wild will choose a kennel in an out-of-the-way place, where they are unlikely to be disturbed, and this sort rarely hunt for food near their home, but go much farther afield, only returning when they are sure that the coast is clear. Nowadays there are an increasing number of what are often described as 'dust-bin' foxes – foxes that live in the vicinity of towns – and although they are by no means tame, they cannot be classed as totally wild like their country or moorland cousins. They live in artificial, almost zoo-like conditions, and these town foxes will snatch anything within a few yards of their home. The same goes too for vixens, however wild, with a large family to support – they bear anything from three to eight cubs – especially if they do not have the support of a mate. They may well have neither the time nor the strength to travel any appreciable distance in the unceasing search for food to satisfy their ever-hungry youngsters.

So we realise that the needs of a fox are those common to most wild creatures – food, sleep and the urge to reproduce. My grand-father in his book on fox-hunting put it most succinctly: '. . . Hunting days excepted, he parcels out the twenty-four hours after the manner of most predatory animals, even after the fashion of the man–about–town; the nights he devotes to refreshment, plunder, and love, the days to the luxury of rest and sleep, being extremely fastidious as to the warmth and dryness of his bedroom.'

The fact that the fox has to hunt in order to live means that of necessity he has to take exercise, and this in turn helps to keep him fit. For his food he prefers creatures in fur and feathers that he has killed himself, but he is willing to feed off carcasses that have either been killed some other way, or have died through severity of weather. If he lives near a lake or river, he will both stalk and kill aquatic birds and will catch fish and crustaceans. It has recently been found that he eats a surprising amount of grass and wild fruits to supplement his diet.

An inspection of a fox's billett or droppings shows that a large proportion of his food consists of black beetles which he finds in the hedgerows and underneath dry cow dung. The outer hard skin is discarded as indigestible, but I am told that the soft inner part contains something that helps to keep a fox in good condition and free from

The enemy – or perhaps I should say 'our friend' the fox. 'In the summer I loves him with all the hardour of affection; not an 'air of his beautiful head would I 'urt . . . but when the autumn comes then dash my vig how I loves to pursue him to destruction.' Young dog fox (John Marchington)

mange. It has even been said that there is something in it that provides the rich scent that enables hounds to hunt the fox. Mange is a killer with foxes, and there have been epidemics in the past that have wiped out large numbers of them.

Rats, mice and rabbits are also part of a fox's staple food. When keepers see the unmistakable marks of a fox around their pheasant coops, they may be forgiven for not realising that generally he has been hunting for the rats attracted there by the birds' food. There is little doubt though that a fox sometimes likes to vary his diet with something clad in feathers, and it is then that a weakly pheasant or stray hen may well be the victim. One must rise very early to catch a confirmed chicken stealer, and often a search for the culprit carried out later in the day results in an innocent fox paying for the misdeeds of an erring brother. Unfortunately, once a fox becomes an inveterate hen-roost thief he is then an incurable criminal, and is not content only with satisfying his immediate needs, but kills for the sake of slaughter when he finds himself in the middle of a bunch of terrified birds.

I have been told that foxes have been known to push hedgehogs into water to force them to unroll themselves, and then snap off their heads. Somehow they manage to turn the creature inside out thus avoiding the skin and the prickles and, in the same way, they get inside a rat's tough skin.

A fox will bury food just like a dog burying a bone. But unlike the dog who often forgets the hiding place, the fox leaves some portion sticking out of the ground, and generally returns later to unearth his buried treasure. He will kill a cat, and dead cats have often been found in a fox's earth. I personally think that a fox will eat a cat, but I know many people disagree with me.

Before studying the behaviour of a hunted fox, let us consider its height, which is only about fifteen inches to the shoulder. As this means he only comes about up to our own knee, his view of the general lie of the land is bound to be very restricted. Things that we would use as landmarks, especially when we are mounted on a horse, remain unseen to him, and so the fox's landmarks of necessity will be a nearby hedge, a ditch, a gateway, a tree or even just a track. From close observation it is evident that he knows his way about his own terrain in the most intimate detail, and it is also evident that he remembers everything he passes, however small and apparently insignificant.

When he is forced out of his own immediate territory, he finds himself totally and completely lost. With hounds close on his brush he is therefore forced to run blind, so to speak, and will often go straight past places that contain safe earths did he but know. Even a fox of great intelligence is not likely to think that a strange wood will offer him refuge when he is being pressed by hounds, so on he runs, and it is then that he is most likely to be killed in the open. Another reason why a hunted fox generally skirts a covert may be that he senses that if he went inside he would not be able to hear sufficiently well.

Though there is considerable difference of opinion among the experts, I think that a fox is capable of enough intelligence to put two and two together and to realise that as he himself hunts by his sense of smell, it must be his own scent that is now making him the prey. However, when he runs down a road, although he may be trying to leave as little scent as possible, it is just as likely that his feet hurt, and the hard road will therefore be easier on his pads! Also it may be one of his nightly hunting routes. I think that when he jumps into a sheep-fold, he is almost certainly doing so in the hope that the strong smell of the sheep will obliterate his own scent; but there again, it may be his habitual route.

A fresh fox moves freely with his back straight and his head high. He will stop frequently in mid-stride to take a look round. When he has run hard, his back arches and his head drops – though should you see him, and he spot you, for a moment or two he will go off as if he is as fresh as paint. It is said that a sinking fox drags his brush so that it becomes dusty or muddy, but I do not agree with this theory. Any dirt that has adhered to a brush has got there when the fox has gone to ground and has been dug out, or has travelled through really muddy, deep tracks and more especially through plough country. Stories about a fox 'wet with sweat' can never be true, for a fox, just like a dog, sweats through his salivary glands, panting with his tongue lolling out. He swims well so when he is wet through he may have just come out of water.

I have seen a fox run along the top of a stone wall, and have heard of one running across the backs of a flock of sheep. Although generally a fox will prefer to run down-wind, it is not true that he will not run into the teeth of a gale if he has a particular point in view. Quite apart from the fact that the fox being so low to the ground feels less force in the wind, my father always said that, as the fox uses its brush as a sort of rudder, if he ran with a gale-force wind behind him his brush would swing up over his back thus putting him off-balance.

A fox will lie very still when hounds are near, and I am sure that he knows that by doing so he emits very little scent. I have seen hounds run right over a stationary fox time and time again, thus providing a perfect illustration that underlines the need for a slow and very careful draw. However, the fox is a wild animal and lacks patience, and he may panic and bolt too soon – this has been the undoing of many a potentially good fox.

He will often run into a covert, shift another fox from a good hiding place and take the place himself. Often he will go into a drain and find another fox already there. If terriers are then entered it is the fresh fox that is most likely to bolt, leaving the hunted fox behind, so hounds may quickly roll the wrong fox over, never realising that behind them their hunted fox is making a stealthy retreat.

Once a fox has been hunted he soon learns a thing or two. One is that he must always slip away from the covert the moment he hears the slightest sound of hounds approaching. Often he will withdraw to a nearby ploughed field, lie doggo for a time, returning once more to the covert when he thinks the danger has gone.

Perhaps I should not say so as a Master of Hounds, but it is not always as easy to head a hunted fox as people imagine, especially towards the end of a hunt. If a fox is getting close to an earth he intends going to, it is surprising what hazards in the way of people, whip-cracking and shouting he will face, and indeed seemingly ignore, being driven on by his determination to reach his haven. Nowadays foxes are not as easily headed by cars as they used to be, for vehicles are a part of their daily lives, the country being broken up into a network of roads that carry traffic not only during the day but throughout the night when the fox is afoot. The greatest problem that arises with cars in relation to hunting, apart from the all-too-evident danger of their speed and size, is that the smell from their exhausts tends to foul the line, so that when hounds reach a road they find it difficult to own it, and the Huntsman will probably have to lift them and do some careful casting before they are able to strike the line again.

Although foxes do not share the cat's gift of nine lives, for they are not on the whole very long-lived animals, they are cat-like in the way they can jump and climb. I have many, many times seen foxes far up in trees at Badminton, and there is a very high wall round our kitchen garden that has been a regular run for numerous generations of foxes.

Icy and snowy conditions do not hold the same number of hazards for a fox as they do for either horses or hounds. In the first place, the fox is a much lighter animal than a hound, the average weight

Foxes often lie in trees

being about 13½lb for a vixen and 15lb for a dog-fox, whereas my hounds turn the scales at 50 to 60lb. This means that when the snow is crusted a fox being so much lighter will skim along the top, while hounds with their additional weight find the going very difficult and sink down into the snow. The same applies to ice, for a fox will be able to cross a frozen pond or lake with impunity, whereas hounds would most likely go through the ice and possibly be drowned, and horse followers will be stopped altogether. Foxes manage frozen slopes far more easily than hounds owing to the difference in the conformation of their feet. Foxes are hare-footed with four claws on each of the hindfeet, and five on each of the forefeet, the fifth consisting of a dew-claw which is an aid to them when surmounting obstacles or descending steep and slippery places. They have too a certain amount of hair between their toes, which gives them additional aid when they find themselves in slippery conditions.

The fact that a fox is being hunted does not prevent him from following his natural instincts, and I have often seen him stop to roll in carrion or manure in just the same way he would were he just

My wife, whom I met in the Hunting Field and who has always been a keen and extremely knowledgeable follower of hounds (William Morris)

travelling from point A to point B. However, here again I personally think it quite possible that the fox knows that, by so doing, he is foiling his own scent.

If a fox is hungry, the fact that he is being hunted will not stop him from killing should he find himself in the position to do so swiftly and easily. I have seen this happen more than once, the fox pouncing on a hen or duck and then carrying his prey on for quite a distance before being obliged to abandon it by reason of the pressure that hounds by then are bringing to bear.

There is a difference of opinion as to the relative fitness between a fox and a hound for a long hunt. Some people assert that an animal that has to work for its survival, that has to hunt and kill its own food, will always be more fit than one that depends on its food being produced for it at regular times. I do not agree with this theory, for I think that under a capable Huntsman a foxhound is one of the fittest animals on earth. Fed as he is to his own individual requirements, and leading a life that is run to a strictly regular routine, he is capable of running up to seventy miles in a day. On the other hand, the fox lives a completely hand-to-mouth existence, never knowing where his next food is coming from. Inevitably he feeds at irregular intervals, all his exercise coming from his hunting or courting expeditions. If when a fox is found he has a full belly, he is then in no condition either for a long or for a fast run. Therefore the hounds, having had a good night's sleep, and then hunting on empty stomachs, are bound to have the edge.

What it is necessary to remember, though, is that a fox will often appear to be faster and therefore fitter than hounds, because he is not having to puzzle out a line. What he is doing is running as straight and as fast as he can to a particular objective – unlike his pursuers, the hounds, who can only travel as fast as their noses will allow.

I have noticed that when scent is bad, the fox has more time to turn and twist and double and jink, which makes it twice as difficult for the hounds, who already have the disadvantage of contending with the bad scenting conditions. There is no doubt at all that hounds find it far easier to hunt what we term a 'straight-necked' fox – one that runs straight from A to B – than a short-running twisting one.

It is a fact that foxes are capable of extraordinary bursts of speed, travelling far quicker than hounds over rough uphill terrain. This may of course be a classic example of fear adding wings to the feet so to speak. When a fox 'potters' along, he may be doing so with intent, for it is well known that when he does so he leaves less scent, and I am sure he is well aware of this fact.

I have heard it said that a dead-beat fox does not look back when hounds are near; but time and time again I have been in a position to see a weary fox snatch a quick glance over his shoulder in exactly the same way that we would were we being pursued to the death. After all it takes great control and training to ensure that human athletes save all their energies for their task, and do not waste time or energy in looking back to see how near the closest rival is, and a fox certainly does not receive the benefit of a formal training apart from that provided by his own life-style, being as he is a wild animal constantly on the alert for unwelcome attention.

As I said earlier, when hounds are running hard they must be running more or less blind, their noses being close to the ground, so it is therefore all too easy for them to run over and past a fox that has had the sense to lie doggo. The most likely thing in that event is that the hounds will check, turn back, and with a bit of luck view their quarry as it slinks off a moment too soon, and then it will be rolled over. A good pack that is running for blood is unlikely to make a mistake at this point in the run, and it will be a lucky fox that will make an escape.

Often on the way to the Meet, one smells the rank and unmistakable scent of fox. This does not necessarily mean that a fox has passed that way within the last few minutes. It is more likely to denote the limits of a particular fox's territory, as he will mark it out rather like a dog does in his own garden. What it very often does herald, alas, is a bad scenting day, for it means that the scent is rising and evaporating quickly.

The fact remains that it is a fox's cunning that often saves his life, and I shall always contend that his very cunning is a sign of his high intelligence.

3
The Foxhound

I think it is true to say that the dog is the only animal with which we have mental contact and understanding that transcends the need for any but the most elementary words and gestures, and the likely reason for this is that man and dog developed their intelligence together at the same time. Another interesting thing is that both men and dogs are pack animals, and that may be the basic reason why such deep bonds have always existed between them. Remembering this, we only have to take a step further to see how the whole development of a working pack of hounds came about; for obviously the dogs, instead of following one of their own kind as they would in the wild, came to look upon a man as their leader – in this case the Huntsman.

Packs of hounds have existed for many hundreds of years, and I was very interested to read the following passage written by Xenophon, the celebrated Greek writer and cavalry general, in about 400 BC:

> If your hounds are as I have described in appearance, they will be strong, light, swift runners, bright eyed and clean mouthed. In hunting they ought soon to quit beaten tracks, slanting their heads towards the ground, smelling at the tracks and drooping their ears downwards, and while they dart glances this way and that, and wag their tails, they should go forward in a body towards the lairs making many deviations. When they are actually near the hare, then they should give the sign to the huntsman, by running about much more quickly than before, signifying by their eagerness, and with the head, the eye and their entire change of carriage, by their looking towards or at the hare's hiding place

and moving their bodies forwards, backwards, and sideways, by their obvious joy and delight, that they are near the hare. They should pursue the animal unremittingly and steadily, with a great noise and barking, penetrating everywhere the hare does, and run quickly and vigorously after him, twisting with him this way and that, barking furiously.

Although this was written over two thousand years ago, leaving out some of the twisting and turning and substituting the word 'fox' for 'hare', it would not be a bad description of a pack of modern foxhounds.

Peter Beckford, whose book *Thoughts on Hunting* is a classic for all time, said of the hound in about 1770:

Let his legs be straight as arrows; his feet round, and not too large; his shoulders back; his breast rather wide than narrow; his chest deep; his back broad; his head small, his neck thin; his tail thick and brushy; if he carry it well, so much the better. . . . Such young hounds as are out at the elbows, and such as are weak from the knee to the foot should never be taken into the pack. . . . I find that I have mentioned a small head as one of the necessary requisites of a hound; but you will understand it is relative to *beauty only;* for, as to *goodness,* I believe large-headed hounds are in no wise inferior.

I find my grandfather's remarks made at the turn of this century on the subject of hounds, extremely interesting too:

. . . but the hound must possess nose, stoutness, speed, courage, and a number of valuable qualities which may be briefly summed up under the head of intelligence. If a hound be handsome so much the better, of course; but the best hound is the one that works best, not the handsomest. There is something particularly pleasing to the eye in the sight of a level, symmetrical pack. To breed a pack of hounds, perfect alike in appearance and in work, is, however, the labour of a lifetime. Nose and stoutness are the two things which the breeder of hounds should first of all seek to obtain, and experience shows that no two attributes are more distinctly hereditary.

(above right) Palmer '59, one of my most famous stallion hounds
(below right) Bert Pateman, my previous Huntsman, preparing to take hounds out on exercise in the early summer

Now let us go on further into the twentieth century, and see what that great expert in all matters appertaining to hunting, Lord Willoughby de Broke, had to say:

> The modern foxhound is bred, or ought to be bred, with a sound constitution, contained in a graceful, elegant, and symmetrical body of a size which is neither bulky nor insignificant. This type has now held the field for about one hundred and seventy years. . . . Let us try to describe him in a little more detail. He stands not less than twenty-three, and not more than twenty-four inches high. He has a lean head, rather conical than flat, with a delicately chiselled muzzle; dark, full, luminous eyes, denoting keenness and intelligence; close-lying ears, small and pointed. His long neck, with the line of the throat quite clean, is supported by sloping shoulders, at the foremost point of which his fore-legs are set on, with the knees near to the ground, plumb straight whether viewed from the side or the front. His feet are round without being fleshy, with the toes close together. His fore-ribs are deep, but not so widely sprung as to push his shoulders forward. The upward curve of the under-line is not unduly pronounced, even when he has not been fed for twenty-four hours. His muscular back is flat and straight right up to the point where his feathery and delicately curved stern is set on. The thighs are wide and muscular, supported by straight hocks to the ground like his knees. His coat is smooth, glossy, and so supple that you can pick up a handful of it from his back and see it glide back into its place the moment it is released.

The first thing I look for myself when either judging or just looking at hounds, is the breastbone. If it juts out well, then it follows that there will be good sloping shoulders behind. I do not like the toes of the front feet to turn in too much, for that in turn leads a hound to be 'out at the elbow' which must impair his speed. Hounds must be strong and muscular with a good neck and shoulders, well sprung ribs and straight legs. They must have good hindlegs and quarters and a straight stern and I like a dog-hound to stand about twenty-four inches high.

Lord Lonsdale, who was my godfather, would never keep a dog-hound unless he were quite level in the back; but many judges nowadays like to see a slight arch. The main necessity, however, is that the hound should have a strong back, for without muscles here everything else goes for nothing. It is difficult to judge a hound unless you are standing over it, but by and large a flat-sided hound is almost sure to be a bad-winded one. Speed and strength alike call for great length from hip to hock, and as little as possible from hock to foot. Although I like a dog-hound to look like a dog-hound and abominate a snipey head, the best size of all, of course, is the one that is most often at the front on the line of a fox, and with a great cry!

When talking of hound-breeding, it is necessary to begin at the beginning and think first of the choice of a bitch for brood purposes. She should, of course, be a first-class physical specimen with bright eager eyes, a clean shining coat, alert and brisk in her movements. Most important of all, she must be 'bred right'. May I say here that before you ever consider breeding, you must start by getting to know the *Foxhound Kennel Stud Book* inside out and, if you have no personal knowledge of breeding, do not be afraid of going for advice to someone who does. It is up to you then whether you take it or not. I always think it wiser not to listen to too many people, as conflicting advice is always liable to lead to confusion.

Hounds from Hunt kennels are bred in the main for performance, so it follows that the stock chosen should have proved its scenting ability, cry and all the essential working qualities. However looks

Gimcrack '70 who was champion doghound at both Peterborough and Honiton in 1972

must also come into the general picture, and most Masters of Hounds are endeavouring to produce as level a pack as they can – that seem to be, to use Peter Beckford's words, 'of a family'. Beckford also said: 'I advise you to adopt the size of hound that suits your country best. There is, however, a certain size best adapted for business, which I take to be that between two extremes; and I will venture to say that such hounds will not suffer themselves to be disgraced in any country.'

Stamina is absolutely vital, as hounds are called upon to run such enormous distances – anything from sixty to seventy or more miles in any one day. Not only do they have to be capable of these feats of endurance, but they must be fit and ready to go out and do it again two or three days later, and so on throughout the season. Their constitution must enable them to hunt regularly and as often as need be. A hound of poor constitution that will not eat up at night and is only good for one day a week is an expensive and unsatisfactory animal to keep.

Again I quote that pundit of all time, Peter Beckford:

The dog you mention. In his second season I wished to test his line, so gave orders on 1 September that he was to hunt every day (four days a week) until he dropped. He never missed a day, finished in April and has more condition than any other hound in the kennel. One day in February, as we came to the foot of the Downs, he shot ahead of the bitch pack and led them up the hill. After his last day's hunting he weighed 2lb more than in September – muscle!

A bitch must have good nerves and temperament, and I will never breed from a nervous one, though I must say here that it is very important to assess whether any trace of nervousness can be accounted for by environment or recent happenings. The really nervous bitch has a certain look about the eye that is unmistakable, but such animals are few and far between, and I myself fortunately have rarely come across one.

Aggression is another trait to be avoided, and although there is bound to be a certain amount of this in a hound's general make-up, there are distinct limits. Bitches that attack each other repeatedly should not be bred from. I also like to choose brood bitches that have good brains, as this trait is likely, though unfortunately by no means certain, to be passed on to their progeny. Whatever else, they must never run mute. What is known as 'the cry' in fox-hunting circles is of the utmost importance in a pack of hounds, for without the sound of their voices, the Huntsman would sometimes not know precisely where they were running, and would therefore find it virtually impossible to keep with them.

Above all, I study the pedigrees. This is an essential for all would-be hound breeders – indeed, the same rule applies to the breeder of any kind of animal. When a particular dog-hound and a particular bitch have produced an exceptional litter, I tend to repeat the process, as it is not often a fluke.

That foxhounds must have a good nose and tongue goes without saying, for what is the use of a beautiful hound if he cannot hunt? One is reminded of the old maxim that a pack can only hunt as fast as their noses, and how true it is. I do like to be able to hear them at their work. When I became Master of my own hounds, though I knew that they were as stout as ever, I did feel that they lacked cry. To remedy this defect, I successfully introduced new blood with Sir Ian Amory's *Tiverton Actor* and Mr Isaac Bell's best lines in the South and West Wilts kennel. 'Ikey' Bell used Welsh blood, and this is a national infusion that has helped the cry of many other packs of hounds as well as my own.

There is always a great deal of controversy about in-breeding and line-breeding. In-breeding implies breeding from parents that are related in the first two generations; the term line-breeding is used when the ancestor common to both appears on the pedigree twice or more in the third, fourth or fifth generation. I do both line- and in-breeding on occasion when I want to establish in the strain the blood of an ancestor who had high qualities that I am anxious should be carried down permanently to his descendants.

Lord Henry Bentinck hunted the Rufford and Burton countries for thirty years, and his great edict was *hold on the line*, which was a constant reminder to breed to the line and not to the individual. He also said that the secret of his success was to breed a great many hounds, and then to put down a great many. If you can afford to follow his example so much the better for the future of your pack, but it has been said with a great deal of truth that it is harder to maintain excellence than to achieve it. The tyro taking on a first-class pack is bound to have severe misgivings, but in a long-established pack there are bound to be old and well-tried kennel lines, and these are sure foundations upon which to build future hopes. So all in all, if you are a novice you will do best to stick to the general breeding scheme that has been carried on in the past if it has produced good results. If you have taken over a really poor pack, then you will have to study the whole subject and go for lines that you know for certain, or are told on the best authority, have proved successful in other packs.

Good sires can provide a change of blood and bring fresh qualities. They can produce strong constitutions, conformation and speed, nose, tongue, drive and the ability to turn with the fox, activity and soundness, and the probability of longevity in their stock. Do not, however, expect all these qualities from one stallion-hound, for he is a hound and not a magician! I do not believe that a single hound can or ever did 'make a pack', and he certainly cannot

do his stuff without the proper bitch. But undoubtedly, given the right material, he can go ahead and leave his mark. It is indisputable that the most successful packs result from a breeding policy with the fewest and least drastic changes.

It is when you are trying to build up a pack from drafts of all shapes and sizes, which obviously you want to work as a pack and not as individuals, that the conformation of your brood-bitches is all-important. Big hounds, medium hounds, and small hounds

Brian Gupwell, my Huntsman, and Denis Brown, my first Whipper-in, bringing hounds back to Badminton from exercise

cannot possibly be expected to work at the same pace or in the same way, so once you have established the type for which you are going to aim, the selection of brood-bitches can begin. In these particular circumstances, you must pay particular regard to the conformation of your bitch, and not select her for her performance alone if you are ever going to achieve any sort of levelness in your pack.

My proudest possessions are my old-established female lines for, if they were once bred out at Badminton it would be quite impossible to replace them. My stallion hounds are, of course, used by many other packs, but it is my brood-bitches on which I rely to carry on the general looks that do make my pack all 'of a family'.

We generally cover our bitches that come in season in January, as early whelps are desirable, and thus we expect our litters in March or early April. They then have the summer ahead and can go out to walk that much sooner. If however I am particularly anxious to breed from a very special bitch, and she does not come in until later in the year, I do not let that deter me. I would recommend anyone taking over a pack of hounds to follow Peter Beckford's once again admirable advice, and see to it that late whelps go out to what you believe to be the best walks.

You must never get the idea, however, that you can correct faults by breeding to opposites. You are more likely by so doing to accentuate the very things you want to get rid of. If you think your bitch is a bit long in the back, do not make the mistake of putting her to a short-coupled stallion-hound, for out of a litter of six you are likely to get a long one, a short one, and four other rather nondescript whelps. The chances too are that if you get one of the type you want, when you come to breed from her she will throw back to her dam, producing a large litter of long whelps, so there you are – back to square one.

Now we come to decisions that must be firm and may sound ruthless, for hounds should not only be even in their looks but, if they are to show good sport, ideally they should be even in their performance. By these standards, if one hound outruns all the rest, then he must go. Equally, one that consistently falls back has to be drafted. A skirter – one that runs round the edge of the body of the pack – will have to be culled, as must one that runs mute, which to my mind is the worst fault of all. This stringent rule also applies to a babbler – a noisy hound that throws his tongue too often and at the wrong time. The hound said to 'dwell' or 'tie on the line' is a hound so pleased by the scent of the fox that he almost sits down to sing a song of glory about it. This is an unpopular trait, and one that many

It needs a lot of experience to sort out a group of puppies. Here I am judging the Whaddon Chase puppy show in 1971. Albert Buckle is still the Huntsman

people agree should be eliminated from a pack. It often occurs with trencher-fed foot packs.

There is another thing about which I have read, though I must admit I have never personally come across it, and that is conceit which can amount to a vice. It is said that this can happen when a young hound, having shown early brilliance, has heard the pack cheered on to him too often, the result being that he may want to get away on his own without speaking. Thus, when he suddenly gets the urge to throw his tongue, he has the great pleasure of hearing the pack cheered on to him, whether this is justified or not. It is also said that too much use of a young hound as a stallion is liable to produce the same effect.

The worst vice, which fortunately is rare except in rough Moorland country when the hunt staff cannot keep with hounds, is sheep-killing. A young hound may well come across a sheep caught up in wire when there is no one there to discipline him. As the sheep bleats and struggles, that hound will become interested and bay at the sheep. Very soon other hounds will appear on the scene, and it is in the general ensuing excitement that the unforgivable crime takes place. Once hounds get a taste for sheep-killing it is well-nigh impossible to eliminate it, though I have heard people say they have effected a cure by tying down their young hounds and driving a flock of sheep over them. Some Moorland packs keep sheep about their yards, and even take them out on exercise with hounds.

A story is told that an old ram with big horns was left in a certain kennel with young hounds, who took not a jot of notice as long as there was someone watching. Come the morning however there was a different tale, for all that remained of the ram was a fine pair of horns and a few pathetic scraps of wool. (There was once an unpopular Huntsman who disappeared in the same way!)

4
Kennels

Upon some little eminence erect,
And fronting to the ruddy dawn; its courts
On either hand wide opening to receive
The sun's all-cheering beams.

E. Somerville: *Notes of the Horn*

There cannot, of course, be any hard and fast rules about the layout or the management of kennels, for so much depends on what is available, individual requirements and prevailing conditions.

Beckford, when describing what he considered to be the ideal kennel, reminded the friend to whom he was writing that:

> ... as often as the mind may alter, and as often as one might change from one kind of hound to another, your kennel will remain the same. It will stand there with its original imperfections, unless it were the object of considerable expense, a memorial to the fact that insufficient thought has been given to its original erection. Even if it is changed, and changed again, it may still remain imperfect, so it is as well to ponder deeply before embarking upon the original building.

This advice remains as good as on the day it was given two hundred years ago – and it goes, too, for any other building or dwelling. The kennels that my grandfather built at Badminton, like the stables, have stood the test of time, as there have only needed to be a few very minor modifications, mainly of modernisation concerned with the introduction of electricity, and the provision of garages. The hunt staff houses have, of course, been fully modernised.

Another thing that Beckford stressed was the need to build kennels that would be large enough for future needs from the outset, as to add to them later could well be prohibitively expensive. I agree with him, although my only criticism of my own kennels is that I would like to see our yards much smaller. However as their size is irrevocably governed by the position of eight-foot high walls, there can be no thought of doing anything, except possibly to subdivide them inside.

My grandfather wisely said that the first thing that must be taken into account is the financial means of the builder. Then must come the consideration of how large a hunting establishment is required. He pointed out that the kennels at Goodwood had cost several thousand pounds – which must have represented a considerable fortune in those days – and those at Woburn, the seat of the Duke of Bedford, had a frontage of 150 yards. He did not feel that it was in the least necessary to take buildings of such magnificence into account as examples of how things should be done, for kennels that would prove quite adequate for all practical purposes could be built on a much more modest and frugal scale, often with existing outhouses and barns being brought into use. However, I do not think that Beckford would have agreed with this advice for he said in another of his letters:

> It is true hounds may be kept in barns and stables; but those who keep them in such places can best inform you whether their hounds are capable of answering the purpose for which they are kept.

Beckford went on to say that cleanliness is the first essential for a hound, for on that rests his whole performance, his working ability depending on his nose. If that sensitive organ is surrounded constantly by a stench, the hound cannot be expected to do his job properly. I agree with this absolutely, for if a pack of the best bred and best trained hounds in the world were expected to pig it together as best they might in some dirty outhouse or diseased barn, then obviously their efficiency would very soon suffer, as indeed would their general well-being as a whole.

Undoubtedly, if the money will run to it, by far the best plan is to have buildings put up for the specific purpose of kennelling hounds. But every pack cannot expect to have perfect kennels, as each Hunt is obliged to cut its coat according to its cloth. However, what can and must be fulfilled are the necessary requirements of cleanliness

My hounds in kennels

and order – and these standards can be maintained even in Beckford's despised barns and stables.

On whatever scale, or to whatever plan, kennels may be built there are three essentials to be observed. It is imperative that they should be dry, that they should be airy and that they should be warm. My grandfather was adamant about this, saying that sweetness and light were as vital to the proper well-being of the hounds as to their master: '. . . in proportion, they are even more so; for, while some men do certainly in this world contrive to get on without them, we are very sure no hound can.' On the other hand, he did not hold with any artificial heat, preferring to rely on the bodily warmth that is so readily transmitted from one animal to another. In my kennels now we have almost tile-smooth solid concrete benches with a wide pipe running through the centre of the block. The body warmth from the hounds heats up the concrete, and the pipe acts as a conductor of this heat – an ingeniously simple idea that works excellently in practice. These concrete benches are far more easily and quickly cleaned than the old-fashioned slatted benches on hinges that used to take a man several hours to scrub out thoroughly.

I have included a plan of the kennels at Badminton which has hardly altered since my grandfather's time. The hounds' bath at the entrance is used to this day, all the hounds having to go through disinfected water as they come in either from hunting or from exercise.

We now have a set of whelping kennels running up the Park side of the grass yard that lies to the right of the main entrance, where all the brood bitches go just before they are due to whelp. As soon as they can be moved, a time that may vary from one day to four, they are switched to a hound paddock that lies between the kennels and the stables. Here the whelps remain, with plenty of room to run about, until they go out to walk.

On the further side of the whelping kennels is a place that we now use as a sort of sick bay, for it is essential to have a place where hounds can be kept apart, or even quarantined if necessary. Animals often make a quick recovery from minor ailments in solitude, and it is imperative that they should be kept on their own and away from others if they are seriously ill. Anything slightly infectious will run like wildfire through such a big establishment.

The places shown in the original plan as whelping kennels are now used as spare kennels where terriers can be kept, or as extra 'hospital' accommodation. Sometimes an odd hound that has been brought back late from hunting is better left there rather than run the risk of disturbing the rest of the pack by putting him in with them.

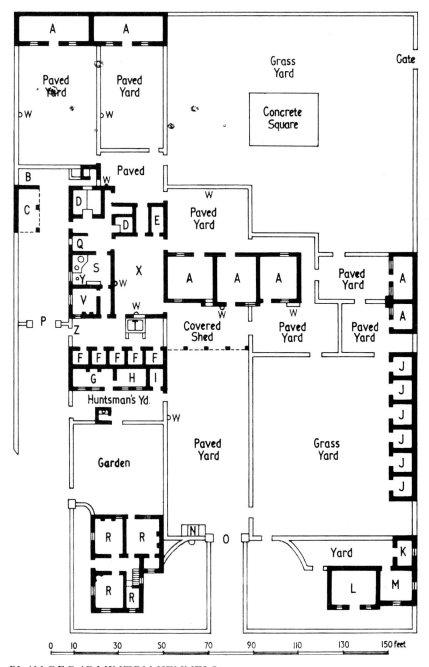

PLAN OF BADMINTON KENNELS

A *lodging houses;* **B** *bones store;* **C** *larder;* **D** *stores;* **E** *store closet;* **F** *terrier whelping;* **G** *garage;* **H** *garage;* **I** *wood store;* **J** *bitch whelping;* **K L M** *kennelman's house;* **N** *hounds' bath;* **O** *principal entrance;* **P** *waggon entrance;* **Q** *refrigerator;* **R** *Huntsman's house;* **S** *boiling house;* **T** *spare;* **V** *kennelmen's room;* **W** *water taps;* **X** *feeding house;* **Y** *spare;* **Z** *general entrance*

39

A hound puppy brought in from walk late at night can be put there on his own until the morning when he can be introduced to his new companions in the light of a new day, which will probably give him a better start than if he had been pushed in at dead of night. My grandfather had the door of the young hounds' kennel kept open all day, as he thought it most desirable for them to have enough room to exercise themselves when they were first brought in from their walks, before they became a part of the pack and were subjected to kennel discipline.

Although our boiler-room is in the same place as it has always been, instead of the porridge on which hounds were fed we now use flaked wheat which is scalded the night before, then next day mixed with thoroughly boned meat that has been chopped up and cooked on a large bottled-gas stove the previous day.

The feeding of a pack of hounds is of necessity determined by what is available, and while we find flesh difficult to come by, the proximity of Bristol Zoo accounting in part for this, there are many packs that still are able to feed raw flesh. Raw flesh takes much longer to go through a hound than cooked meat mixed into a porridge, and therefore it is customary to feed them far less often, and in fact, although it sounds cruel, hounds often hunt after a fast of thirty-six hours to ensure that their stomachs really are empty.

The greatest innovation that we have made, in common with many other Hunts all over the country, is to have a massive deep-freeze installed, and this we did with money raised by our Hunt Supporters' Club. It has revolutionised the feeding arrangements as it means that we never have to turn gifts away. We therefore do not meet the problems that have always up to now beset a hard-pressed Kennel-huntsman, in that he was often obliged to resort to such devices as keeping the meat immersed in water, which made it spongy, or covering it with sulphur, or trying to obtain sufficient ice. Deep-freezing is by no means a modern invention though, for in the grounds at Badminton there are no fewer than three ice-houses which were used in the olden days for preserving food, and it is probable that the one nearest to the kennels was used for hound meat.

Originally there was provision for 'the Huntsman's cellar'. I can only suppose that that was used to house beverages for the staff in the days when no breakfast was complete without a flagon of ale!

(right) The Master of the Tipperary on the way to the Meet (J. Meads)
(overleaf) The Beaufort near Bowldown Wood. This is not a posed picture and,
perhaps for that reason, I am not in it

5
Hound Management

As soon as it is light, winter or summer, the Kennel-huntsman or whoever is in charge opens the kennel doors, and the hounds are all taken out for fifteen minutes or so. Their absence gives the kennel staff the chance to clean out the sleeping quarters, and provide fresh bedding if it is used.

While they are out the troughs are filled, and when the hounds are brought in again those that are not hunting that day are fed, at about 7am in winter. After their meal, they are turned out into the yard, where they are left to themselves until about 10 o'clock, when they are again taken out. They have another run at about 4 o'clock and after this, in some packs though not in mine, a few delicate feeders are given another meal. The pack that has been hunting that day have their meal when they come in, as they will have been hunting on empty stomachs and will be ravenous by then.

My Huntsman never puts all the food into the trough at once. He divides it into thirds, and after all the hounds have had a go he removes the greedier ones that always get there first and never go short, and lets the more shy ones have a second turn. He watches them all closely the whole time to make absolutely certain that each hound has had sufficient; if he thinks a particular hound needs feeding up he includes him in a small lot that are allowed to have three goes at the trough. He prefers to do this rather than to give them a second feed, as he feels that extra feeds are liable to make for fussy feeders. If a hound knows that he is going to get some more later, he will not bother with the first feed.

The most important time of all for hounds is the summer, as that is

Brian Gupwell with my hounds in front of the house

when the fitness they will need for the ensuing season is built into them, and they are taken out for exercise four times a day. When they are outside in the yards they play and lie about under the trees, eating grass which is very good for them, and earth too. It is noteworthy that sometimes a hound puppy will show a great desire to eat horse dung – a desire shared by puppies of all breeds. I am told there is some element in it that is of great benefit to them and many breeders of pedigree dogs actually buy horse manure for this specific purpose.

In the summer then the hounds are at first exercised on foot, those that have just been brought in from walk going out on couples with a more experienced hound. A month or so later they are taken on mounted exercise, going about six to eight miles at first, the distance becoming longer and longer as time progresses and they become more fit. As I said, this summer exercise is all-important, as it gives them steady preparation for the rigours of the hunting season.

Hunting is not exclusively the 'sport of kings' – it can be enjoyed by all. These are the North Lonsdale foxhounds, a trencher-fed pack, coming home after a seven-mile hunt (W. Wilkinson)

Not the least of the pleasures of hunting is often the beauty of the surroundings. Here Will Finlay, Huntsman to the College Valley, blows for his hounds amid the majestic Northumbrian hills (Frank H. Meads)

Obedience has of necessity to be the cardinal rule in the kennel, and if possible this should be obtained by the power of the voice alone. I always feel that the whip should be a symbol of authority rather than a weapon for punishment. Naturally this is a counsel of perfection for it is necessary to use the whip on certain hounds.

Puppy Walking

The puppy walkers are the life-line of the Hunt and, next to the farmers – very often one and the same as the puppies mostly go to farming families – we owe them the greatest debt of gratitude for they are a special race of people. They come along to the puppy show year after year, and show no rancour if their charges do not gain a prize, for they are always so happy to see them in the ring. Year

47

after year they go on walking puppies for the sheer pleasure of it and to help hunting, in the same way that their fathers and their grand-fathers did before them and, with luck, their sons will after them. The ideal puppy walker is a farmer, but that does not preclude others from offering and having their services accepted for what I consider to be a most rewarding job.

The function of the puppy walker is to start the education of the young hound, and food will be provided for several months that will save the Hunt a great deal of expense. The Huntsman is the person qualified to provide a list of things that any particular puppy should have as a necessary part of his diet; but obviously milk, meat, vegetables and biscuit meal must provide the basis of what is required to build substance into a puppy.

Your puppy will have been ear-marked when he comes to you – a number on one ear and the initials of the Hunt on the other. He will also already have been named, the intitial of his name generally indicating his breeding, and most likely being the same as that of his sire. It is up to you to try to the best of your ability to teach him to know his name. You must never resort to a pet or nickname, as that will effectively defeat the object of the exercise. Then you must see that he comes obediently when called. This is easier said than done, for foxhound puppies are the most mischievous things that God has put on earth to try us all – it is fortunate that they are also endowed with more than their fair share of charm!

Given half a chance, they will set to work and systematically demolish half the contents of your house and garden. Whatever you do, you must *never* let them set a paw inside your saddle room. Ideally, the stables are the place for them, and preferably a place where they cannot chew their way out. A family dog is a good companion, especially a long-suffering one that will stand a certain amount of nonsense and then will put the impertinent little upstart sharply in his place. That lumbering, charming bundle will soon become a leggy, disobedient bundle of trouble unless he is treated firmly from the start. In the long run it is much kinder to be strict, as otherwise the puppy's eventual transition from stable yard back to the kennels is going to be a very difficult one.

If it is safe to do so, the ideal exercise is with horses as soon as the puppy's legs are strong enough to stand up to the sustained running involved. There can be no hard and fast rule about when to start this, but the Huntsman will be round from time to time to see how your charges are getting on and he will advise you, not only on this, but on any other problems that may arise. My Huntsman

The North Lonsdale hounds out at exercise in the wonderful landscape of the Lake District (W. Wilkinson)

Hound exercise has to be carried out in all conditions. The hunt terrier has joined the North Cotswold on this wintry morning (Frank H. Meads)

A couple of whelps at five days old (Nicholas Meyjes)

More snowy conditions, when the Old Berkeley were obliged to hunt on foot
(Sport & General)

always gives the puppies their injections himself; this means two visits, a month apart, and so he is able at the same time to see how they are getting on.

A foxhound puppy is just like any other young animal – a mixture of all sorts of traits: he can be curious, perverse, charming, disobedient, wilful, perhaps shy, possibly a little too bold for his own safety. But he thrives best in an active environment where he sees people and things, and where there are constant comings and goings with all manner of excitements to watch, all of which add to his general education and help him when he returns to kennels to become one of the pack.

A good puppy walker will take note of the particular character of the puppies he has that year, and will be able accurately to pass on his observations to the Huntsman. This information will be of the greatest help, for the Huntsman is going to have a young hound back at the kennels that may present a very different picture from the bold little character that was afraid of nothing in the familiar surroundings of the farmyard.

When a puppy goes back to the kennels, it is rather like a rebirth, for everything is strange, and the poor creature is going to have to learn a totally different way of life. The first and the most important lesson he must learn, and quickly too, is absolute and instant obedience. If some general principles of obedience have already been instilled into his brain, he is going to find that 'rebirth' a far easier transition. I do not mean that it is necessary to train the puppy to walk to heel or anything fancy like that; but it is clearly going to be a great help if he has learnt to follow a horse quietly and confidently, avoiding its heels, and also a good deal about the dangers of motor vehicles. My Huntsman always suggests to puppy walkers that their charges should be shut up when there is going to be a lot of tractor movement about the farmyard, as there is bound to be during hay-making or at harvest time. In hot sunny weather a hound puppy will often lie under a vehicle seeking the welcome shade with tragically fatal results for, alas, he tends to blend into the background and become invisible, and it is only too easy to move a tractor without realising that a puppy is fast asleep underneath it.

He should also have learnt to be an avid and quick feeder, an ability he will need when he returns to kennels where first come is first served, and it is every hound for himself. Mind you a good Kennel-huntsman or Kennelman will watch the feeding habits of his

'I'm not really asleep. I'm just thinking of what devilment I am going to get up to next!' (W. Wilkinson)

Better known for his commentating at all our great horse shows, here Dorian Williams, Master of the Whaddon Chase for many years, has a word with the hound puppies he is walking (Nicholas Meyjes)

charges closely and, as I explained before, will see to it that no individual ever goes short.

Your young charges will stay with you from the age of two to three months until spring the following year, and your reward will come when you see your rascals showing themselves at the puppy show sometime between late spring and early autumn. If they get a prize, your heart will swell with pride and, even if they do not, you will still be able to take enormous pleasure in the knowledge that you have performed a great service for your Hunt.

What the puppy walker must bear in mind when watching his particular hounds in the ring is that many factors determine which puppies are to be prize winners on any given day. One of these is bound to be the taste of the particular judges; another is that it is all too easy for a puppy to be slightly off colour one day and as fit as a fiddle another; and he may be as bold as brass in his own territory, but miserable when he is put on display. Inevitably too some puppies will have developed much more quickly than others, and although their more late-developing brethren may not win a prize at the puppy show one summer, they could well be material for Peterborough the following year after having had a season's hunting, when the symmetry of their conformation will have been put to the test and their muscles will have developed. Who knows? That is one of the delightful imponderables about it all.

One of the signs of good judges is that they will take just as long over each entry, whatever its merits or demerits. They are fully aware of exactly how much it means to the dedicated puppy walker to see his own hound really looked over properly. Nothing is more dispiriting than to see the puppy to which you devoted so much care, and for which you were bound to have had high hopes, dismissed from the ring after just a cursory glance. This, of course, goes for all judging in every field, not only at puppy shows. Even at family dog shows, every entry deserves its full share of the judge's attention.

The puppy show is to my mind a small way in which a Hunt can say thank you for the services that are given so generously and at no small expense nowadays. It serves a dual purpose, for it enables members of your Hunt to see the young entry, and also provides the opportunity to return past hospitality from other Hunts.

Sir Hugh Arbuthnot hunting the Cotswold hounds on foot during bad weather. Here they are seen waiting for a terrier to be run through a drain (Fox Photos)

6
Hound Shows

Although I know that there are considerable differences of opinion as to the value and merits of hound shows, I myself, for many reasons, am very much a supporter and protagonist of them. For one thing, I believe very firmly that they set a standard and give encouragement to the smaller packs to whom the opportunity to send a hound to say Peterborough or Honiton provides the greatest impetus in their programme of breeding. I have found also that those who speak loudest against hound shows are likely to be people who cannot produce anything good enough to be shown.

Another extremely good job that hound shows do is to give members of the general public, who may or may not already be interested, the opportunity they would never otherwise have to see the best hounds that are being bred at any given time from all over the country. Packs are brought from far and wide to the big hound shows which therefore also provide the opportunity for both Masters of Hounds and hunt servants to meet each other and exchange ideas and views, and this is bound to produce a good effect on general morale. I think it is particularly valuable for hunt servants to have the opportunity to move about in this way, for their free time is bound to be limited by the very nature of their work. They are so much tied to one place by their responsibilities which, as already seen, are by no means confined to the hunting season alone but extend into all the months of the year. A Huntsman who is not

(above left) Queen Elizabeth the Queen Mother making much of my champion doghound, Culprit, at Peterborough, 1976 (Frank H. Meads)

(below left) The Marchioness of Abergavenny presenting me with the cup at Ardingly, where my Beadle was champion doghound (Frank H. Meads)

Bert Pateman, my then-Huntsman, with his Whipper-in, Will Ockwell, showing off Whipcord who had just been made champion doghound at Peterborough (Sport & General)

only capable of showing good sport, but can also produce and show hounds at the bigger shows (an art in itself) it something quite exceptional, and a man of that calibre is greatly to be valued.

Anyone coming to a hound show without knowing what is going on could well be excused if he were to think that all those men in brightly coloured coats had gone mad as they wave their arms about and gesticulate. Seen from the waist upwards it is a crazy sight – one which would baffle the panel of judges who used to sit on a programme called 'What's My Line', where they had to guess from a short mime the occupation of their contestant.

A hound with a doubtful neck will be persuaded by a good Huntsman to show every inch of it by his holding the biscuit, which is the lure, about knee-high. Conversely a bad showman can make a hound with an excellent neck look as if it has no neck at all simply by holding the biscuit so high that the hound goes back on his haunches pointing his nose in the air, thus wrinkling his neck back into his shoulders. The true artist at the job of showing anticipates the judge's every movement, never being caught when he suddenly spins round on his heel to take another look at the hounds standing behind him. But I must say that, speaking as a judge myself, many of the antics and subterfuges are really unnecessary. Quite frankly I can tell for myself whether a hound has a good neck, shoulders or anything else; equally I can spot a fault pretty quickly whatever the devices used to deceive, if you can really call it deceit. At any rate, we have kept the brush and comb out of the hound rings, reserving them for pedigree dog shows! May I somewhat immodestly say that only judges who are not of the highest calibre could be hoodwinked in such a way?

However, it is essential that hounds should be shown properly if they are to be shown at all. To this end the Huntsman and his aide, the Whipper-in, must be in complete accord throughout. But although the experienced Whipper-in in this highly specialised field will be at one with his Huntsman if they are in the ring, such close co-operation is sometimes unnecessary, for an occasional Huntsman has a very special gift of showmanship. I would like to finish with a passage taken from *Come and Hunt* written by Charles Willoughby, who was undoubtedly one of the greatest experts on hound breeding who ever lived, his pedigree books being perfect examples of accurate industry and attention to detail:

> Each time the huntsman brought in entries, he walked quickly to the concrete slab in the middle of the ring, his hounds nuzzling his hand. Once there, the huntsman took up his position and the hounds took up theirs. No movement at all from man or hounds; they were as statues. When let loose, the hounds showed their movement to perfection, and on the slightest sound of a high-pitched whistle they returned to stand in front of their huntsman, with eyes for nobody else. They all left the ring after the final judging as happy as when they entered it, win or lose. That huntsman never seemed to need an assistant, for he had brought hound control to the point where it borders on magic; yet controlled as those hounds were, what impressed me so greatly was the spirit of good humour and good fellowship between them and their huntsman.

It is that same spirit of good humour and good fellowship existing between hounds and their Huntsman that makes all the difference to the sport shown in any country which, after all, is largely what hunting is all about.

My Joint Master and more than right arm, Major Gerald Gundry, going to draw in the days when he hunted hounds (Fox Photos)

7
The Running of a Pack of Hounds

It is difficult for one who has been raised in a family whose successive generations have been intimately connected with hunting, and who have always lived where the whole way of life is geared to the sport, to realise that there are bound to be whole sections of people who know nothing at all about it. These unfortunate beings have never had the wonderful experience of going out in the half-light of an early September morning and seeing hounds outlined against the red and glowing background of the rising sun, nor experienced the thrill of the view holloa, the find, and eventually the sight of hounds all together going away well on their fox.

Such people are bound to think of hunting only in the light of the biased accounts they have read in the newspapers or seen on their televisions – and these accounts inevitably will be very much in favour of the sport or very much against it. Hunting does not lend itself to any middle-of-the-road attitude. Naturally too they will not be in a position to understand the titles or the functions of the people in the hunting field.

We more fortunate beings who have been brought up to it do not find the terms that are in constant use at all technical, and it is difficult for some of us to realise that a newcomer may be at a loss. I myself can readily see that for someone who has always lived in the middle of a town, even a short visit to the depths of the country is almost like going to a foreign land. How can he be expected to know why the letters MFH after a name still carry a prestige above many other high distinctions, especially if the men (or women) concerned have also gained for themselves reputations for knowing what they are doing, and have perhaps even hunted hounds, and built up a good kennel? It is not a mere conceit to place those letters after a name.

How can the townsman possibly be expected to know that all those taking part in the hunt are not 'huntsmen'?

Many people think that such distinctions are out-of-date traditions, but believe me, they rest on very real foundations. A good Master of Hounds is in part born, but is also in part made, and it needs a man with very special qualities both of courage and of humility to make a success of a position that is by no means a sinecure. The running of a pack of foxhounds is a continual and unending process; it demands selfless and unceasing attention from a dedicated band of workers on one hand, and constant loyal and unswerving leadership on the other.

Nowadays, with money short and labour so expensive, there is inevitably considerable interchange among the various duties that arise in stable, kennel and in the field itself. While Masters have always hunted their own hounds, the general tendency nowadays is for far more to do so as amateurs, employing a Kennel-huntsman to look after the hounds and to hunt them when they themselves are unable to do so. Keen and knowledgeable members of the field act as unpaid Whippers-in, thus saving the Hunt the expense of employing a professional. However, in spite of all this, the traditional structure is still maintained, and I will try to explain what it is all about.

First, it is necessary to state categorically that the prime purpose of fox-hunting is to kill foxes in as controlled and efficient a way as possible. Being vermin that cause considerable losses to farmers, poultry-keepers and game preservers, they are bound to be treated as such and many and varied will be their fate; but no method of killing will be as humane as that provided by a well-conducted Hunt.

The way we do it is to hunt them with a pack of hounds, and this requires a degree of skill, knowledge and courage that is not immediately obvious to the uninitiated. The hounds need to be disciplined and controlled, or they would soon run amok and cause more trouble and damage than the quarries they are pursuing. Hence the need for a man in charge who is called the Huntsman. The Huntsman is assisted in his work by one or two 'Whippers-in', so-called not because they actually physically whip the hounds but because they help to control them and make them pay attention to the Huntsman and one of the means they use is their whip, which they crack or flick around a hound to make him sit up and do what he is told.

There are, of course, many other mounted men and women who ride to hounds and, although a number of them do so only for the thrill of the cross-country ride, the jumps and the excitement, there is always a basic core of people who come out because they enjoy watching hounds work and take a delight in the venery, ie the art of hunting. In spite of all the propaganda there has been in recent years to the contrary, very few come out to see a fox killed. In fact I would make so bold as to say that no one who hunts seriously is interested in the actual kill. Should there be people who are so perverted, it is most unlikely that they will achieve their ambition very often, as it is extremely difficult to maintain a place in good hunting country that will enable the kill to be witnessed consistently by members of the Field. Even the best men to hounds only see foxes killed three or four times at most in a season.

When my grandfather published his book on hunting at the turn of the century, he made no mention of the duties of a Master of Hounds. He probably thought it superfluous, as he would have expected people with packs of hounds to have been brought up in the hunting tradition, and therefore to know what they were doing. His whole book was probably intended as a treatise and guide as to how to carry out the job successfully. Lord Willoughby de Broke said in 1920:

> No-one is too good to be a Master of Foxhounds. If he be gifted with the average endowment of tact, administrative talent, power of penetrating character, and all other attributes that form the essential equipment of a successful public man, so much the better; but he should at least be reared in the atmosphere and tradition of country life, fond of sport for its own sake, a good judge of horses and hounds, *and the possessor of a remarkably thick skin.* [The italics are mine!]

However, times have changed in the last fifty to sixty years, and things are totally different nowadays. Many people who do not necessarily have the sporting background of our immediate ancestors are gallantly taking on packs of hounds.

The first thing I would impress on an aspiring MFH is that to undertake these duties is not only extremely expensive but overwhelmingly time-consuming. But I imagine nobody in his right mind is going to do so without a considerable amount of thought and, by the time 1 May arrives when he enters into his duties, he will surely have weighed up the expense and the time involved fairly accurately.

When a change of Mastership is indicated, the procedure followed nowadays is that first the Hunt Committee get their heads together and discuss the possibility of asking someone local to fulfil the role. Sometimes they are successful, and are able to make an appointment without resorting to advertising – except by the local grapevine that exists in every country community, and more particularly in hunting circles. If there is no suitable local candidate, the post is advertised in the sporting papers – indeed, some packs have a stipulation written into their rules and regulations laying down that when one Master retires, in cases where there are two or more Joint Masters, the others must stand down, and the post be advertised before new arrangements are made.

The candidates will be told what is expected of them in regard to the number of days' hunting each week, how much money the committee can guarantee, and roughly how much the potential Master will need officially to put into the Hunt. Only then will he be able to make an assessment of how much the venture is likely to cost, bearing in mind the horses, transport and staff that he will need.

Under the system followed by most Hunts, the hunt servants are considered to be employees of the Master or Joint Masters, who therefore have complete authority over them. This avoids any possibility of a disagreement as to policy in the field, which might arise if the committee had any similar authority.

Each country varies, of course, but by and large it is the 'hidden' expenses that are the ones a potential Master should beware of – for believe me there is a constant demand for donations to this and that, prizes for whist drives, tombolas, terrier shows; and the incessant entertaining that forms a very necessary part of the job. People who come to discuss hunt business must be offered a drink, and you will find tea, coffee and whisky flowing ad lib. Then there is the petrol for the frequent visits that have to be paid all round the country. There is no end to the incidental expenses, and at the present time with prices soaring so fast, it is difficult to see what the future will be.

The Master in fact is ultimately responsible for the welfare of his country, and he is required to direct the sport in the field. This will involve him not only in hunting say three times a week, but also in regular visits to farmers and local landowners, in keeping an eye on the coverts in and out of the season, and in attending a host of activities which take place mostly in the winter evenings when perhaps he would prefer to put his feet up. These activities will all be directly or indirectly concerned with the Hunt, either for raising money or endeavouring to promote the goodwill which is such a necessary part of the Hunt as a whole.

His task will be made easier – or possibly more difficult – by the calibre and character of the Chairman and members of the Committee, his Joint Masters and that of the Hunt Secretary, who is a key pin to the success of a pack these days. I myself have had the good luck to be born to the task, but that does not mean that I do not appreciate the difficulties of others who have not been given such a close insight into the job from earliest childhood. I am also aware that I am additionally privileged by following a long family tradition, which meant that I picked up the reins of what – to use a modern idiom – was a going concern.

In general, the Master has to work through the agency of his Secretary and that of the Committee, who in turn must consult him before they make major decisions. There are very few sole Masters of Hounds these days, so the Joint Masters must have temperaments that fit in with one another, and each should be prepared to look after a single aspect of the running of the Hunt. It is most important that an appearance of unity should be presented to the world at large, and any differences that arise must be settled in private.

It is vital too that the Master should know exactly what is going on in his country, rather as a good headmaster knows, without appearing to look, what is happening behind the scenes in his school. If the Master keeps an ear well to the ground, much potential trouble can be prevented by his taking swift action at the right time.

One of the main tasks of a Master of Hounds is to engage the hunt servants, and this is a difficult and hazardous proceeding. I have heard it said that it is easier to choose a wife than a Huntsman! If you know a particular man and have the opportunity to study the way he works, you are indeed fortunate if you find that he is free at the time you want him. Otherwise you will be obliged to rely on hearsay, though you will be wise to check on what you have heard by going to watch the man at work. If you can possibly spare a week or more in this way, so much the better, for it is very difficult, well-nigh impossible, to make an accurate assessment of either a man's virtues or his faults in one day, which may or may not have been a particularly good hunting day.

What you must watch for is the ability of a Huntsman in the field to mark and bear in mind afterwards the exact spot where the leading hounds lost the scent. Then comes his power to keep his hounds together, well in front of him, with their noses to the ground; all this without relying too much on the help of his Whippers-in. There is no doubt at all that there is something radically wrong if you see a Huntsman constantly in front of his hounds, poking about with no particular reference to the place where they threw up, and then sending off one of his Whippers-in to collect odd parties of hounds. He is not the man for you.

It is difficult, perhaps I should say impossible, to find someone who combines all the qualities that are desirable for a first-class Huntsman, and you will almost certainly have to settle for the man who comes nearest to your original specification. It is important that he should be one whom you personally take to, and also who you think will suit your country. Do not forget to take a look at his wife, for their relationship and the way his home is run is bound to have an effect on a Huntsman's work.

On your voyage of inspection you must, of course, visit the kennel. Beckford said that the kennel should have 'a neatness without and a cleanliness within, the more to tempt you with it'. General cleanliness, order and tidiness denotes a well-run establishment. The inmates should be alert, happy and healthy, and the boiler-house efficiently run with the food thick. I myself would look for signs of sensible economy and would pay particular attention to the general atmosphere, especially among the staff. If they are relaxed and happy, my general impression would be a good one.

Although it is important for a Master to be aware of what is going on, both in kennel and stable, it is also important to remember that once you have engaged good staff, you should leave them alone to a certain extent to get on with the job. But they must know that they can always come to you with any problems, and you must always be seen to back them up in public, regardless of what may be happening behind the scenes. Obviously a Master who is keen on hound breeding and wants to breed an even pack and produce a likely winner at one of the hound shows, will want to supervise the breeding arrangements himself; he will therefore find it necessary to visit the kennels more often than one who is content to concentrate on the pure hunting side of things.

Many Masters make arrangements for interested members of their Field to visit kennels at stipulated times during a few weeks in the summer. Although in principle Masters are ever-anxious to promote an interest in their hounds, there are many reasons why the kennels cannot be open at all times, primarily because the regular routine of work must not be interrupted. However, organised visits are extremely valuable as not only do they serve to promote a greater interest in the hounds generally and give people the opportunity to learn some of their names, they also help the hounds themselves. It is surprising how much a shy young hound will 'come on' when he sees plenty of strangers before he is introduced to the hurly-burly of the actual hunting field.

Such visits also help the Huntsman, who is able to make a shrewd assessment of his future Field, and may be able to decide who will very likely prove a useful ally in the field when he may be hard-pressed and in need of reliable assistance or accurate information. They also provide him with additional income, as it is customary to tip the Huntsman when visiting kennels. It is also customary to tip him when you are given a trophy, such as a pad or mask, or when a child is blooded.

The choice of other hunt servants is a different matter. Although they have to be chosen in part for their general qualifications, they also have to be chosen for their ability to fit into an established pattern and for their willingness to learn. Obviously they must be prepared to carry out orders from the Huntsman immediately and without question.

On the matter of staff generally, do not forget to give praise where praise is due, for that always engenders good feeling and all-round harmony. Everyone likes to be appreciated! Should you have to administer a reprimand, let it be in private. Nothing is more distasteful than people rebuking servants in front of others, however justified a complaint or reprimand may be.

I am not going to touch on the mounting of the hunt servants in this chapter, but do remember the value of buying local horses. I quote R. E. Egerton Warburton:

> *And should his steed with trampling feet*
> *Be urged across your tender wheat,*
> *That steed, perchance, by you was bred,*
> *And yours the corn on which he's fed.*

While you probably take a natural interest in the horses hunted and bred by your farmers, it is absolutely vital that a Master should take an interest in the puppies and their walkers. This sort of personal touch is of far more value even than silver cups, cream cakes and tea on a fine summer's day.

Before ever hounds are taken out, the question of earth-stopping has to be considered. Some Masters, and I am one of them, prefer to deal with all aspects of earth-stopping themselves; others leave it to their Hunt Secretaries. I personally think that this can only be done if the secretary hunts every day in the season from beginning to end. Even so, the Master and also the Huntsman must know the earth-stoppers and where they are to be found. In non-Moorland countries, earth-stopping is of the utmost importance, as it can make or mar a day's sport. To go to a covert and then to draw it blank because the earths have been left open is a disaster, as it affects the whole day's sport as well as leaving one open to criticism and even ridicule.

It is equally disappointing if a fox runs to ground just as hounds are settling on to the line. If the fox finds an open earth after a good run, that is quite another thing, for no one can be expected to make an entirely accurate prediction as to which way a fox is likely to go – it can only come from a combination of knowledge and guesswork. Moreover, no one in the world can tell how far the fox is going to run. Constantly running to ground is bad for man and for beast, though I am aware that it is something that has to be accepted in certain areas where the general terrain often makes it impossible even to reach the earths, and where they are so extensive that no amount of stopping would be totally effective. The whole question of earth-stopping is so important that it is dealt with separately in Chapter 14.

Come August, when the harvest is being gathered in, our thoughts turn to cub-hunting, which is the pivot on which a pack of hounds revolves. It is no exaggeration to say that during the cub-hunting time a pack is made or marred. Technically speaking, the cub-hunting season is the Master's season, and people who come out mounted are coming by invitation only so that the Master is under no obligation whatsoever to show any sport. This is the only way whereby he can have a free hand to carry out the necessary training of his hounds without having to 'show sport' to his Field.

The object of cub-hunting is to educate both young hounds and fox-cubs. As was said earlier, it is not until he has been hunted that the fox draws fully on his resources of sagacity and cunning so that he is able to provide a really good run; this ability to run fast, far and use to the full his crafty brain is, in fact, his defence against pursuit. Cub-hunting completes the education of the previous year's entry of hounds and makes a start on the education of the young and unentered ones. Puppies cannot be of proven value to their pack during the first season, and it is not really until the end of their second cub-hunting that you can start to assess them accurately and judge whether they are going to be reliable and steady members of the pack, and tell where their individual talents lie.

The young hounds and foxes are not the only ones, believe me, who derive benefit from the lessons they get during those early mornings in August, September and October. They are invaluable times for everyone, and more especially for keen young people, to learn. I myself never cease to find out something new, and I am a fairly old hand at the job!

We always start cub-hunting the moment the state of the harvest allows, and continue almost daily until 1 November. Even though the ground may be as hard as iron, the training can continue, for there is no need at this time of year to take the horses out of a trot, nor in fact to go far at all, for a long, fast run is certainly not the object of the exercise.

I try to be out cub-hunting as often as possible myself, and the ideal thing is for the Master to be out every day. I do realise that nowadays many Masters of Hounds have commitments that prevent them from doing so, but it is only by personal and constant supervision that you can be absolutely certain that a definite system is followed and no liberties are being taken. On bad scenting days, the Master needs to be extra vigilant to see that no unorthodox methods are followed, and he must insist on that extra bit of perseverance being taken that will ensure ultimate success. Never lose sight of the fact that one really well-beaten cub killed fair and square is worth half a dozen fresh ones killed the moment they are found without hounds having to exert themselves in their task. It is essential that hounds should have their blood up and learn to be savage with their fox before he is killed. A sleeping cub killed by two or three enquiring hounds is of no use whatsoever to the rest of the pack, who will only wander up after everything is over to see what has happened, and nothing will have been learnt.

In small places undoubtedly cubs will have to be held up, and it is better to do this than to go home without killing anything. The orthodox method, and the one we pursue, is to visit the strongholds first and then to stay there all morning, as this is the very best way to teach perseverance to a pack of hounds. This essential quality of perseverance must, in the main, come from above. In the first place it must be shown by the Master, and he in his turn has then to transmit it to his Huntsman, and so on right down to the hounds themselves. Young hounds fortunately, like most juveniles, are extremely receptive and open to learning.

When you think that every cub must surely have left the covert, it is still worth drawing back again over the old ground, just in case a tired one has lain down again in the hope that he will be left in peace to continue his slumbers. This is often better than starting all over again to tire a fresh litter, for undoubtedly it is of greater value to hounds to finish a long morning by re-finding and killing a tired cub with a good cry after about fifteen or twenty minutes than perhaps not to kill at all.

You must take no notice of critics, and you must be prepared to keep to the same ground all morning if necessary. After all, this is a vital time of schooling for all concerned. As often as not your prey will tend to creep back into the covert and therefore will be found again on foiled ground. Tired cubs lie very close in thick hedges and deep ditches, so the drawing back must be even more painstaking than the first visit.

For the first four weeks, there are two reasons why you must keep your hounds in the covert. Firstly, puppies will learn to depend on their older companions and go more quickly to a cry in the covert than they will in the open. Secondly, they are obliged to use their ears, noses and general intelligence, and are not so likely to lose interest in the job in hand through all the other diversions that are more readily available in the open. You must always remember that they are still puppies, and puppies like to play, and even a butterfly flitting past can be of fascinating interest when boredom is setting in. Their ability to concentrate is limited, and therefore it is most important that their interest should be retained. If the cub-hunting is carried out in proper style, by the end of September they will have learnt to hunt as a pack without the help of holloas, and without needing assistance when their prey jinks and they over-run the line.

It is easier for the hunt staff to keep with their hounds in covert, though it becomes more and more difficult as the season progresses. If hounds do get away without any hunt staff to check them it can spell disaster, for without guidance from their Huntsman the puppies will inevitably follow the older hounds. Then, when there is a check, perhaps a hare will jump up and the youngsters will be off after it, and everything they have learnt up to then will go with the wind. It takes weeks to put right mischief that has been done in this way, and sometimes it is impossible ever to remedy the damage that has been done.

If hounds do get away on an old fox, they must be stopped, but this must be done in such a way that they do not think they have done wrong. The best thing is for the Huntsman to make every endeavour to be with them when they first check. The moment their heads are up, he can get them away from the line, catch their attention and bring them back to the covert at a pace that will ensure they cool down before they are asked to start work again. In general hounds should not be asked to draw with their mouths open, that is to say when they are hot and their tongues are lolling out, as it impairs their scenting ability. It really is not fair on them, as they cannot possibly give of their best.

By October, when the country is getting more and more practicable for hunting and if the puppies have been well schooled in the coverts, they should at last come out if it is absolutely certain that they will come out altogether as a pack, and be allowed to pursue their cub for a sharp burst or two in the open. This will teach them to negotiate the fences, and will improve their general condition by opening up their pipes. I do not mean, though, that they should be holloaed away on the first fox that leaves the covert. That to my mind is a great mistake, for it is almost certain to be an old dog-fox which will take them so far from home that it will not be possible to return that same morning to deal with the remaining cubs. A golden rule to remember is that during the cub-hunting season hounds must always be made to find their own fox.

Now we come to the exciting day of the opening Meet. This is when the Master not only has to think of his hounds, but it is now that he has also to take note of his mounted followers. In other words, this is when the Field come into the picture to claim their rights to a good day's sport, and you can take it from me that they are not nearly so manageable as a pack of hounds! However, if the Huntsman's horn and voice can be clearly heard, and are intelligible in covert, then the Field should have a rough idea of what is going on. They will then be less likely to stray off to try to find out what is going on, thus running the risk of spoiling what might have been a good run. Would that the Field *were* as obedient as a pack of hounds! Once they have got away, it is almost impossible to bring them back. This is where the duties of the Field Master need to be examined in some detail.

His first and foremost duty, as his very name implies, is to control the Field. This, as I have already intimated, is a good deal easier said than done. Many a promising gallop is spoiled, and therefore many a fox's life is saved, by the pressure of a field of horsemen advancing too fast just at the crucial moment when the hounds require both the time and the room to manoeuvre, as they check and then spread out to cast themselves efficiently. The words of Peter Beckford once again come to mind:

Gentlemen, [and doubtless had he been writing today, he would have added ladies] when hounds are at fault, are too apt themselves to prolong it. They should always stop their horses some distance behind the hounds and if it is possible to remain silent, this is the time to do so.

The art of controlling a large Field seemingly effortlessly – and believe me it is an art – is not given to many. Firstly the aspiring Field Master must know the country intimately, for without this knowledge it will be well-nigh impossible for him to lead a Field of perhaps two or three hundred, making sure that they are in touch with what is going on most of the time. It is essential that he should be mounted on a good horse that is not too green. He must also have a really practical knowledge of hunting, for while he has to do his task with the precision of a cavalry leader, at the same time he must appear to be relaxed. What is all-important, though, is that he must have complete authority, and be respected for it.

He is helped in his work indirectly by the Huntsman, for if the latter's horn and voice are always clear, the Field will know when they can stand still with no fear of getting left. If people cannot make out what is happening in covert, sooner or later they will start to creep up to try to see for themselves. Once this has happened, it becomes almost impossible to regulate them into some semblance of order again – rather like that terrible little game when you have to persuade a dozen little steel balls that roll about all over the place to go into twelve shallow holes.

The following, which was contained in a speech delivered at Peterborough Hound Show in 1889, fully illustrates what I have been trying to say:

> To my mind the prevailing fault is the *silent system*. If a huntsman goes into a big wood and changes his direction without some noise, his men cannot tell where he is, or his hounds either, and then the hounds are driven about without knowing where to go. You had much better hear the cheery voice of a huntsman than the harsh rate of a whipper-in . . . Wire fences have destroyed the fun of riding across country, and the silent system the cheeriness of running in covert.

If the cardinal rule should be that the Field knows what is happening, then it is vital that the Field Master himself should be completely informed. Quite stern authority and discipline have to be the rule at all times, though I may say that the most successful Field Masters generally manage to temper this with a considerable amount of personal charm.

It must be remembered that seldom are all the riders collected in the same field, and it is the forward pressure on either flank that causes the most trouble. The tendency for the Field to trickle round on either side is even more noticeable where a Field Master has the habit of holding them up in gateways, for this has much the same effect as the damming of a flow of water in the middle – inevitably some will escape on either side. Therefore manoeuvring is best done in the open for the most part, with the gateways being used only at times of special emergency – and then there must be someone reliable to control each flank. People have to be persuaded to go through in as orderly a manner as possible, having regard to the fact that most of them are worried lest their horses should be kicked in the general mêlée.

The first task then of the Field Master is to gain the confidence of his 'public', and in order to do this he must never let them down. He will have therefore to take the greatest care that the Field should never find themselves placed at a disadvantage because they have taken heed of his orders, or next time they may well turn a deaf ear to his commands.

Another vital fact to remember is that foxes do not always run straight ahead and, when they make a sudden turn, it is most important that a group of thoughtless people should not then be found to have over-ridden the line. It is as well to bear in mind that nearly every time this happens the same persons are likely to be the offenders. It is better not to fly off at them in the hunting field, because abuse never helps when blood is hot and tempers short. It is far better to wait until you can have a quiet word with them later, or even write them a line a day or two afterwards. There is no point in going out of your way to make enemies, for no one likes to be humiliated in front of others, however well deserved the rating may be. It is important, too, at the beginning of the day to curb the ambitious spirits who would follow people who have been sent off to do a particular job. Before you know where you are, half the Field has set off in pursuit.

·So tact, charm and firmness combined with a thick skin and a great knowledge of hunting are the qualifications for a successful Field Master.

8
The General Organisation of the Hunt

The business side of most Hunts nowadays is run by a Committee with the usual officers: Chairman, Vice-chairman, Secretary, sometimes a Treasurer, and a number of members drawn from local landowners, farmers and other people who either have an interest in the Hunt or who are able to give valuable service to it by virtue of their specialised knowledge – just like the members of any other committee in fact.

Each Hunt has its own set of rules, but the main concern is always the financial aspect, which assumes more alarming proportions with each ensuing year. The Committee and the Master or Joint Masters have to foot the bills, but the actual paperwork involved is done by the Secretary and/or the Treasurer who are responsible for sending the cheques and for keeping a set of accounts which is presented in the form of a balance sheet before the members of the Hunt at the Annual General Meeting.

In the first place the Committee give the Master or Joint Masters what is called a guarantee – that is they undertake to provide a specific amount of money for the following year – and in turn the Masters themselves are asked to put up a certain sum, which of course varies from country to country. Before making the guarantee, an assessment has to be made at the beginning of each hunting season as to how much is going to be needed to run the Hunt for the

Here I am having a word with our Hunt Secretary, Major Ronnie Dallas, and a journalist, who wrote under the pseudonym of 'Loppy Lugs', at a joint Meet with the Berkeley on my seventy-third birthday

following twelve months, and it is in the light of this that a figure is arrived at.

The money required to run a Hunt is raised each year in a variety of ways. One of the principal sources is the subscriptions paid by those members of the Field who hunt regularly, and who are therefore entitled to call themselves subscribers. In most Hunts, after a probationary period of perhaps two or three seasons, they are invited to become members, and in many cases this membership permits them to wear the Hunt Button and perhaps a coloured collar. In the case of my own Hunt, the wearing of the Button and that of my Blue and Buff – which latter is a separate thing altogether – is by my own personal invitation. It is as well to check on the rules that prevail when you are a newcomer to a Hunt.

The many other ways whereby money is raised to help swell the coffers include caps taken from visitors, donations, and money raised by the Hunt Supporters' Club. The Hunt Supporters' Club can certainly be described as the financial life-line of many Hunts in the British Isles, for without these bodies of hard-working well-wishers, it would be almost impossible for them to be run at all. Supporters do not need to be members of the Field, and in fact generally they are a body of people who never had the good fortune to take an active part in a chase mounted on a horse. However, happily they share with an ever-increasing number of people all over the country a love of hunting, and most of them are avid and knowledgeable followers of hounds in cars, on motor bicycles, and on foot. They carry their interest into practical terms by running a variety of functions to raise money for their Hunt. Most of these are extremely entertaining social occasions, and range from whist drives, dances and draws, to sponsored rides, auctions and even camel racing!

The Hunt Secretary

One of the mainstays of any Hunt is, of course, the Secretary. In his capacity as an honorary officer of the Hunt he is responsible both for the liaison that must exist between the Master or Masters and the Committee (he must call and attend all committee meetings and take the minutes) and for the maintenance of good relations between the Hunt and the farmers over whose land they ride.

His job will involve him in what is sometimes an overwhelming amount of work, because in addition to dealing with a mass of correspondence and a great deal of visiting, strictly speaking he is also expected to be out mounted in the hunting field every time hounds meet. Many Hunts are obliged to have two Secretaries, as they find it impossible to appoint one man who can spare sufficient time to do the job properly. He needs to be a minor diplomat and, if he is wise, he will do a lot of visiting of farmers during the summer months when he can go as a friend and without cap in hand, thus building up good relations. He will thus not only get to know all the farmers, but he will be able to make a shrewd assessment of their particular circumstances and general habits.

On the financial side, his first responsibility is to collect all subscriptions which officially fall due on 1 November, the exact amount being fixed each year by the Committee, and naturally varying from Hunt to Hunt. Some Hunts prefer to have a rate for each horse taken out, others for each day hunted by the rider, and many more charge an all-in rate per person or family. In my own country, every class of subscriber and his position in the country is taken into account, and I am glad to say that one authoritative book I consulted when writing this one described our subscription list as 'a model of fairness'.

In common with many up-country packs, visitors only come out with my hounds by invitation. We have very few subscribers who do not live in the country and as the Fields tend to be very large, especially on Saturdays, we cannot permit their numbers to be swelled even further. However, in many places further away from London, visitors are made very welcome, as the money they pay as a cap helps with the ever-constant financial worries that beset and threaten to overwhelm small struggling Hunts. Indeed, in such countries, car-capping provides an enormous source of income.

Car-capping is a slightly controversial subject, however, for I feel that once money has been taken from people they are entitled to a certain amount of freedom of movement. In our part of the country this is not practicable, owing to the network of main roads. So if people have not been asked for a donation, I feel at liberty to ask them, if necessary, to go away. However, many of my car followers are also members of my Hunt Supporters' Club, and many too come from quite a long way to enjoy a day with hounds, and they are made extremely welcome. If people are going to follow hounds in a car, I think it is important that they should understand that they must abide by many of the same rules and regulations as the mounted members of the Field. I personally do not think that this fact is impressed nearly enough on car followers.

(overleaf) Our rule of 'no horse boxes at the Meet' has been broken on this day at Tetbury (Fox Photos)

To do his job properly, the Secretary needs to be a very special person, for he has to get on with each and every farmer and to smooth over the many and varied difficult situations that arise in the field from day to day, and he must keep on good terms with the followers. All this in addition to paying all the stable and kennel bills for fodder, shoeing, veterinary work, saddlery, repairs to the establishment, to say nothing of dealing with the wages each week, PAYE and VAT!

As he has to collect caps from visitors and Field money from all mounted followers, he has to indentify strangers at the Meet, and collect varying sums from them, sometimes in weather conditions that defy description. Just imagine riding a tricky young horse that you have been lent only that morning because your own steady old hunter has gone lame, on a wet and stormy day, facing a gale-force wind, raising your hat and demanding a number of pound notes from a total stranger on an equally fresh young horse. The money will inevitably become sodden in the downpour, and will then have to be transferred to a reasonably waterproof inner pocket, while both horses bucket round like broncos from the Wild West. And at the end of the day, not only does all the money have to be accounted for – and a good deal of cash is handled – but the Secretary has to wrack his brain and remember the multitude of promises and messages he has received during the course of the day. There are always the people who promise to pay 'next time', or to send a cheque; or, worse still, the man from whom you demand a cap who turns out to be the Master of another pack of hounds, who sent a message the day before which you either did not receive or forgot and who should not, of course, be capped at all.

A good Secretary is a godsend to a hard-pressed Master of Hounds, but in the light of what I have said, you will understand that it is not a job to be undertaken without a good deal of thought, as it is so time-consuming and arduous. However, it also carries with it the satisfaction of a good job well done, and considerable status in the country.

Each Hunt has its own financial arrangement with the Secretary, generally settling his out-of-pocket expenses such as telephone calls, stamps and secretarial assistance. Many also make him an allowance for the maintenance of horses, for transport and other expenses.

9
The Huntsman

It is almost impossible to describe the duties of a Huntsman on paper, but I will make an attempt to tell you from my experience what I think they should be, though obviously they are bound to vary from country to country according to the conditions that prevail.

First I think I should make it clear that there is more than one type of Huntsman. There are the professionals and the amateurs, but it is of the former with which this chapter is primarily concerned, writing from the viewpoint of a Master who does not now hunt his own hounds.

In the old days, many landowners owned and hunted their own packs of hounds, and were responsible to nobody but themselves, and thus were able to be as despotic as they chose. Nowadays, though in vastly diminished numbers, there are still private packs of hounds hunted by their owners who do not have to concern themselves with the edicts of committees.

The amateur Huntsman who is most familiar in the hunting field nowadays is the keen young man who is fortunate enough to have the talent, knowledge and skill to be in demand, and who, although he does not of course have a salary, has most of his expenses met out of the general Hunt funds about which I shall be speaking later. I myself, and many other amateur Huntsmen of my close acquaintance started our careers in our early twenties, and indeed many young men gain valuable experience with packs of beagles during their schooldays. I must make it quite clear that an amateur Huntsman necessarily has a totally different approach to his task from that of a professional, as he is able to talk to the other officers of the Hunt on equal terms and is not, of course, a servant in any sense of the word.

When speaking of any sort of Huntsman a passage written by Lord Willoughby de Broke voices my feelings entirely:

> The primary idea that the Huntsman should bear in mind is that the hounds should leave the kennel in front of his horse and remain there all day, except when he is riding well away from them on a flank for the purpose of manoeuvring them . . . It is not consistent with their dignity for the Huntsman to ride away from them at his own pace in silence, and for them to be rudely ordered to follow him by the whipper-in scolding them from behind.

By no means do the duties of the professional Huntsman begin and end in the hunting field because, as you will have read in a previous chapter, hound-control begins early in the summer when the Huntsman first gets to know his charges. By saying this, I mean he really has to know them through and through: their names and appearance are primary and obligatory knowledge, but he must also be fully aware of their varying foibles and failings, as well as of their virtues; he must be able to pick out their individual voices, and be able to judge whether they are reliable or not; and if the answer to that question is 'no', he must take immediate steps either to teach them or get rid of them, either by drafting them or putting them down.

Naturally all this does not happen in five minutes, but starts in early June with hound exercise when, first on foot and later mounted, the Huntsman will take his hounds on what can perhaps best be described as long, disciplined walks during which he is able to observe the behaviour and general reactions of each individual hound.

He will already have talked to the puppy walker, and if it has been what I would call a 'good walk', then he will have gleaned some useful information. He will also be able to make a very generalised assessment of what to expect of a particular hound from his knowledge of its breeding, for there is no doubt that certain tendencies run in families – that is what hound breeding should all be about. As they are obviously not all intended for Peterborough, the most important thing is to get hounds that are useful in the field and will hunt together as a pack.

My grandfather in his book on hunting lightheartedly says:

> The huntsman having made himself well acquainted with his hounds, and they having got to know him, sallies forth from his kennel, his object being to find a fox.

The Marquess of Exeter encourages his hounds in covert (Desmond O'Neill)

What a masterpiece of understatement! To my mind, there is only one man in a thousand who possesses the ability to command the instinctive devotion of a pack of foxhounds, and to do this he must really love his charges. He must be utterly dedicated not just to their welfare but to their ultimate enjoyment as well of the sport for which they were bred.

Hounds are away! (Desmond O'Neill)

My Huntsman casting his hounds along the side of a covert. The Whippers-in have taken up their positions (Guy & Collier)

It is an interesting fact that a hound gives his affection to a good Huntsman rather than to the Kennelman who feeds him, and it is this hardly won attachment that makes all the difference to the sport that is shown in the country. It is interesting too to note how many good Huntsmen are following a family tradition – though that is to be expected, I suppose, as they will have been brought up to the job from early childhood. I tend to believe that all the really superlative Huntsmen – and there are and have been relatively few – are born and not made. The following extract from *R. S. Surtees* by Frederick Watson illustrates this statement:

> There are three essentials for the higher rank of huntsman. He must be with his hounds, which may mean – apart from wire – some heartbreaking falls, he must have sense to leave them alone at a check, and after, if they fail to pick up the line, he must have an instinct – it is neither more nor less – which tells him the direction the fox has taken. Only one huntsman in a hundred exhibits these three accomplishments.

Talent counts, of course, but any latent talent must be backed up by good sound knowledge, and there is no college where a boy may go to learn the art of being a Huntsman. It all has to be done from observation and from general experience in Hunt service, with family tradition a great help in this respect. In this as in so many other walks of life, personal experience is the only teacher, therefore a man will probably not become a successful professional Huntsman until he is over thirty. He can then look forward to well over twenty years of active life in the saddle – in point of fact, both my father and I hunted hounds until we were sixty-seven years of age.

It is essential for a would-be professional Huntsman to move about a good deal at the start of his career, so that he can give himself the opportunity of watching the methods of as many people as possible. Thus he will be able to make his own comparisons, and decide for himself what he would have done in certain situations had he been carrying the horn.

It is important that he should keep his weight down, as the lighter he is the easier he is to mount, and therefore he will have a greater choice of countries. There can be no doubt that the heavier a man is the more expensive it becomes to mount him, for it is more and more difficult to find good weight-carriers for the hunting field at a price that is not astronomical, as more of them are swept up for show jumping and eventing.

It hardly needs saying that a Huntsman has to be a good horseman, for otherwise he cannot hope to keep with his hounds. He has to be able to use his horse as a vehicle, and ideally he should be the sort of rider for whom all horses 'go well'. The other essential is that he should enjoy good health, have a sound constitution and be physically fit, for otherwise he cannot possibly be expected to do a job that requires him to rise early, be out in all weathers and conditions and to work extremely long hours with very little time for relaxation.

He is second only to his pack of hounds, for without him there would be no sport, and he has to turn out day after day, arriving punctually at the Meet looking immaculate, when in all probability he has already done what would amount to a full day's work in many other jobs. He must have good manners and an excellent memory for human faces, as well as for hounds. He also has to have a good voice and horn. What is more, he has to have courage and complete dedication to duty. I can think of no other walk of life where so many good qualities are required in any one man – and to the ones I have already mentioned must be added honesty and sobriety.

I turn to Peter Beckford once more for a thought on the last quality which may amuse you:

> A huntsman that I once knew (who, by the by, I believe, is at this time a drummer in a marching regiment) went out one morning so very drunk, that he got off his horse in the midst of a thick covert, laid himself down and went to sleep: he was lost; nobody knew what was become of him; and he was at last found in the situation that I have just described. He had, however, great good luck on his side; for, at the very instant he was found, a fox halloo'd; upon which he mounted his horse, rode desperately, killed his fox handsomely, and was forgiven.

I like to see a man who is quiet with his hounds, but whose hounds look at him for guidance constantly and, when receiving a slight wave of hand which expresses his approval, are brought racing to his side. What I cannot bear to see or hear is a Huntsman who seems to think he can command the obedience of his hounds by the loud use of his voice and, even worse, the lash of his whip. In my service the unwarranted use of the whip is followed by instant dismissal and all the hunt servants employed throughout the years at Badminton have known this.

The Huntsman is in a position to command respect and, to my

In full cry. The Huntsman of the Eridge has placed himself strategically to prevent the Field from going over the line (Sport & General)

mind, if he does his job properly, he deserves every last grain. Unfortunately, like all public figures, he is a veritable Aunt Sally, and is open to the widest criticism. If something goes wrong, what easier than to put the blame on the Huntsman? And it is only the genuinely true sportsman who has the generosity of spirit to praise the Huntsman when things go right.

The job of a Huntsman in the field, whether he be professional or amateur, is to show good sport, and give his Field as many good hunts as is humanly possible in a season. When I say 'humanly possible' I mean exactly that, for adverse conditions of weather and scent must always be taken into account.

In his job he is often impeded in many ways, and I would like to mention some, as it may help you to understand more about the problems he faces – and I truly believe you will find that with increase in understanding will come greater enjoyment of your hunting. What I would like to say at this point though is that no Huntsman can give of his best if he knows that half the Field is

87

The Goathland hounds on a good scenting day (Frank H. Meads)

The Duke of Buccleuch's hounds drawing a difficult piece of forestry covert (R. Clapperton)

grumbling about him. No truly good sportsman harbours un-generous and unkindly feelings, and this generosity of spirit must extend to the Huntsman in his truly difficult task, for nobody but one man, the Huntsman himself, knows the exact circumstances that cause him to make a spot decision on his course of action.

Each day's hunting inevitably presents a different set of problems. First and foremost is scent – or perhaps I would be putting it better if I were to say 'lack of scent'. No Huntsman in the world can control scent, and in fact though screeds have been written about it and people never seem to tire of talking about it, I personally think that basically there is nobody who really knows a great deal about the subject. In fact I agree with a certain well known Master of Hounds who said: 'There's nothing so queer as scent, 'cept a woman.'

I can summarise my own knowledge of the subject fairly succinctly into the following observations: Scent will be good when the ground is warmer than the air; but you must remember that this may vary from field to field, as ploughland may be warmer than air at the same moment that grassland is cooler. A sudden fall in temperature just before a frost is a good sign, and I have found that scent is best early in the morning and in the late evening, and on a bad scenting day it often improves late in the afternoon, especially before a frost. It is good on moist ground, and on snow that has fallen before a frost. Strangely enough, it is often good in foggy con-ditions, which causes great problems when making the decision as to whether to let hounds go or not. Scent tends to be better, too, in long grass and heather. Obviously, scent improves if a fox runs up-wind, and it is at its very best just after a fox has been unkennelled, and also when hounds are close to their fox.

Conversely, scent will be found to be bad when the air is warmer than the ground, and just after a sudden rise in temperature. It is also bad in bright sunlight and on very dry ground. It is bad on snow that has fallen after a frost has set in and during heavy rain. Again it is bound to be worse when a fox is running down-wind and when it has been foiled by cattle, horses, men, game, dogs, car-exhausts, artificial manure and so on. Bracken, dead leaves and strong-scented crops do not help scenting conditions, and clearly the scent will get worse and worse the further hounds get from their fox.

I have noticed that when fences are black and sharp on the way to the Meet, I can expect it to be a good scenting day, but beware of a mass of gossamer or cobwebs and a blue haze in the distance – and my heart sinks into my boots when I see hounds rolling at the Meet.

Without scent, there can be no hunt – it is as simple as that. We must remember, too, that the fox is really master of the situation, for it is he who sets the course of the run, and hounds and Huntsman, followed by the Field, have to abide by the line he takes.

Should the Huntsman be drawing an open country, he will draw directly up the wind, or with a good cheek wind. The actual speed at which he draws is bound to be governed to a greater or lesser extent by the stuff through which hounds have to go, whether it be roots, gorse, heather, bracken, fern, or the rushes that are profuse in wet places. Wet places, in fact, are excellent places in which to find a fox, for he will often have searched out a small eminence that is dry where he will lie up either sleeping or watching, feeling himself to be comparatively safe. There is an abundance of food available: water rats, moorhen, ducks and mice, so he has a ready-made on-site larder. Often he will make a warm bed in a thick piece of short gorse a couple of hundred yards from the bog, or will find himself a group of high tussocks of strong rough grass which serves as a comfortable and dry lodge, and there he lies and dozes or watches.

As hounds spread themselves about, noses well to the ground, sterns gently waving, the Huntsman must keep a vigilant eye on them for suddenly one hound may put his nose in the air, sniff and then go first to the right and then to the left. This is an indication that he has had a whiff of the prey, and he will now be making up his mind from which direction that tantalising smell is coming. Then off he will go, probably leaving the bog and setting course for that patch of gorse or bramble a couple of hundred yards away. He will take a turn round this, and will find that he loses the scent when he is on the up-wind side but, as he turns down-wind, it comes back again. Then after a little more sniffing and poking around, suddenly he will throw his tongue, fling himself into the bit of cover and, tally ho!, out will shoot a fox.

I have included this description to illustrate that it is of the utmost importance to allow hounds sufficient time to make their draw, and not to push them on too fast. How many thousands of good hunts must have been missed by too cursory a draw at too fast a pace.

To draw down-wind in open country is almost certainly to start a run at a disadvantage and to get a bad start; for even foxes that have never been hunted before are not going to linger when hounds appear on the scene. They are bound to be anxious to get away as quickly as they possibly can, and if they have been hunted before and know what to expect, they will make their escape even faster.

In enclosed country with large coverts, the same rule of drawing up-wind also applies. Here again, the Huntsman must be careful to go at a pace himself that gives hounds a chance to draw the covert properly. When he comes to a clearing he must go at a good brisk trot, but when it is really thick he cannot go too slowly.

What often happens is that a Huntsman will put his hounds into the covert, and then himself trot away, speaking to them all the time. As his voice gets fainter and fainter the hounds, instead of attending to the job in hand, will stop, lift their heads to listen, and then emerge on to a ride to follow their Huntsman – and then they will almost certainly miss their fox.

In woodland, the Huntsman must reckon to make a noise and to make good use of his voice, occasionally blowing a single note on his horn. What I always did was to use this single note when a fox was not yet on foot, then doubling the instant one had been found. Hounds learn very quickly to move swiftly to this 'doubling'.

The horn must be used too if hounds should chance to riot – to go off on a hare or anything else, or to start to run heel line. Then a discordant note should be blown that amounts to a screech; hounds in common with all the canine species have extremely sensitive ears and they cannot bear a discord of this kind. It is understood by the other hunt staff that if they hear the Huntsman remaining in the same place and blowing a series of discords, then he needs help, and someone should immediately go to him. It may be that he has come across his hounds eating carrion, or perhaps having found a litter of cubs, and he will need someone to help him drive hounds away, and then to get them back to the business in hand.

Large woodlands must always be drawn very carefully and closely at all times, or a fox may easily be left lying tight in some unexpected corner. Small coverts should be drawn down-wind to avoid chopping a fox. A few cracks of the hunting whip and a touch or two on the horn may be enough to put a fox on his feet, and with the down-wind side of the covert clear of horses and people on foot, with luck he should then have a chance of getting well away. Chopping foxes must be avoided if possible, as the object of the exercise is not only to kill foxes, but to kill them by fair means and at the same time provide a good run for the followers.

If there is a chain of small coverts, it is wise to send someone on who can be trusted to conceal himself and to keep a keen watch in such a position that he can command a good view of the country, and yet be far enough to the side so as not to head the fox should he break cover. The moment he views the fox he should gallop back, holding his cap up to attract the Huntsman's attention. Holloaing a long way down-wind is a waste of time, for in all probability the Huntsman is out of earshot, and it also will have the effect of spurring the fox on. In any case, no one should ever follow until the fox has cleared at least two fences.

Once a fox is on foot, then the Huntsman's duties are manifold. He will by now have made sufficient noise inside the covert to achieve the double purpose of pushing the fox on to escape as fast as possible and to draw his hounds together so that they are ready to run. This is the moment when the Huntsman must be as quiet as possible, and see his hounds away on the line as quickly as he can. With any luck, his duty then will be to keep as near his hounds as possible, to make quick decisions and to abide by them. But however craftily a Huntsman may plan to drive a fox out of one end of a covert and hope that a good run may ensue, there is nothing to stop Master Reynard from leaving the covert even more craftily at the other end, and then to proceed to do a complete vanishing trick.

A fox is not only cunning and speedy, but he also knows the lie of the land far better than any human being can ever hope to; and you may be sure that he will use every trick of his craft and knowledge to throw hounds off his scent. He loves to run through a flock of sheep, leaving a frightened baaing flock surging hither and thither. Bullocks too are a great help to him, and his delight is freshly ploughed or heavily fertilised land.

It must be remembered, and this I honestly believe, that the fox has the most acute and shrewdest brain and the sharpest intellect in the animal kingdom, and even though a Huntsman may have two Whippers-in and twenty or more couple of good hounds, he also has a large Field, most of whom, I can assure you, do little to help him in his task.

As the Huntsman sits on his horse, which he must ride as if it were not there, and as the fields, woods and fences come rushing past him, not only must he throw his eyes forward, but throw forward his mind in his task of outwitting his quarry. Is Charlie heading for that big earth that lies on the other side of the far covert, or is he

(above right) Brian Gupwell again exercising the hounds in that frightful winter of 1978–9 (Anthony Del Balso)

(below right) During the 1973 Three-Day Event the hounds were brought round to be inspected by the Queen and some of the younger members of the Royal family (Anthony Del Balso)

(overleaf) The Heythrop hounds. My family used to own these hounds and my forebears divided their time between Badminton and Heythrop during the hunting season. The Heythrop hunt servants still wear the Badminton green livery, that colour normally being the prerogative of packs of Harriers (The Robert Horne Group)

squeezing himself into the drain at the corner of the lane, a nearby barn, a pile of wood, or one of a hundred other likely or unlikely places? The Huntsman's decisions have to be instantaneous, and must of necessity be governed by a multitude of prevailing conditions. In the middle of this concentration, he finds himself in a road packed with car followers, all of whom may be enjoying themselves hugely, but they do not exactly help the poor Huntsman, who must get across the road or along it as fast as he possibly can. Then, to add to his worries, up will come the Field and press his hounds, causing them to lift their heads just when they should have them well down and be concentrating on the job in hand.

It is no good criticising a Huntsman for making a slow cast. Only he knows what he is trying to do, and the pace of his cast must always depend on the scenting conditions that prevail that day. On a poor scenting day, the cast must be slow if it is to be sure, and as quiet as possible to allow the hounds full opportunity to concentrate and, with any luck, hit off the line. When the scent is red hot, then hounds can be swung round in as lively a way as the Huntsman likes.

A Huntsman must apply great and constant concentration if he is to be successful. He has to use his eyes and his ears all the time, speculating and throwing ideas about in his mind. Was that holloa ahead a true one, or perhaps another fox is on foot, or could it even have been a hare? Do those starlings circling above a field of plough denote the course the fox has taken? Are the hounds getting perilously near a road or railway? The list is infinite.

When the hounds are running, the Field, whatever the pace, have a reasonable time to select their line to the best of their own ability, and according to the abilities of their mounts. The Huntsman's job, on the other hand, is to get over the country as fast as possible, and here I must emphasise again that it is criminal of any Master of Hounds to expect his Huntsman to ride any horse but the best that can be produced, whatever other economies have to be effected.

The longer the hunt, the more the problems multiply. It is bound to continue on an ever-decreasing scent, which in turn means an ever-increasing chance of hounds changing on to another fox that may happen to cross the line. The fox's scent comes from just under the root of his brush and, to a lesser extent from his pads, and a change

(above left) The Joint Master of the Ashford Valley (J. Meads)
(below left) A Meet at the Salutation Inn, Threlkeld, in the Lake District, of the Blencathra Hunt, one of the six Fell packs that hunt on foot owing to the steepness of the country. The hounds are mainly trencher fed, and brought to the Meets by the farmers who keep them (The Robert Horne Group)

97

of fox at a late stage in a hunt is very, very difficult to determine. It is true to say that the longer a fox is hunted, the smaller becomes the chance of killing him.

When hounds check, they must be left to swing and cast themselves forward, back and around. This is when the Huntsman needs to draw even more on his reserves of observation and all his intelligence. It is possible that the fox may have been turned by something that is by now out of sight; or it may be that scent has been foiled by artificial fertilisers or something else. The very instant he thinks he has given his hounds an adequate chance of proving the line by themselves, the Huntsman must take a hand and perhaps try a short cast up the wind, followed by a longer one down. The thing to bear in mind is that hounds are more likely to recover the scent and continue on the line if they are given only just sufficient time – and not a moment longer.

On open downland the scent can be blown about by a sharp wind, and hounds just need to have their heads turned into the wind, then off they will go once more.

While he has to keep as close to his hounds as possible, it is important for the Huntsman not to be right behind them, for this has the effect of driving them, and then they very likely will overshoot the line and be unable to make their turns. A Huntsman really needs eyes all round his head, but never more so than when hounds are running hard. He must always keep a good watch forward, for he may see something that might have caused the fox to jink, such as a cur-dog or a single sheep, and this will enable him to act quickly a little later on.

A word about cur-dogs – and any dog met in the hunting field, whatever its pedigree, is known as such. If you do come up to a man with a dog and suspect that it has run your fox, it is highly unlikely that the owner is going to admit that his animal was at fault. Just take a look at the dog and its mouth will tell a story. If it is shut, you will know that that dog is not the culprit, but should it be panting, you will know exactly where to place the blame. Do not waste time, therefore, in asking the owner if his dog has run a fox – just go ahead and ask how far the dog ran the fox, and ten to one the man will be startled into giving a truthful answer. It has been well known for generations, and I myself have noticed it time and time again: a cur-dog will ruin scent and often hounds will never pick up the line again.

However, whatever the problems, nothing can spoil the glorious moment when hounds catch up with their prey especially after a

The Garth hounds getting near their fox (Eric Guy)

The Huntsman of the Fitzwilliam keeping well to the side of his hounds as they run (Frank H. Meads)

good hunt and a long straight run, then: 'And merrily we'll whoop and we'll holloa'! Once your hounds have been fed one fox by their Huntsman, then mark my words, they are his for life, and nothing can be better for them than being allowed to eat the fox they have caught.

Now let us give a thought to what happens at the end of the day's hunting. If it is in the last week of November or early December, in all probability it will be pouring with rain – indeed it will almost certainly have been raining in fits and starts all day. Once the Field has said 'goodnight' (never 'goodbye' always 'goodnight' when you go home from hunting, even at two o'clock in the afternoon), they will make for home as quickly as they can, either heading for their transport or their stables, whichever is the nearer. When they get home, the more fortunate will be able to hand their horse over to a groom and go into the house to have a hot bath and some tea, or perhaps a stronger drink. Many people nowadays do their own horses, but even so that is the end of it. I am not talking of course of the working farmer, who will not only have to do his horse, but will find a hundred and one jobs waiting for him. But he hunts because he enjoys it, and he thinks it is worth the effort that has to be made.

Please give a thought to the Huntsman who has to get himself, his horses and hounds home. Once there, as often as not with some of the smaller packs, he will have to do his own horse – and then he has to see to his hounds before ever he can think of his own comfort. By the time he gets indoors, his clothes will have dried on him, and he will be hungry and tired. He will have a meal, and even after that he will still have to go out again into the cold and damp to attend to his kennel duties before he goes to bed. Then he will be up with the lark to start it all over again.

There is still, mercifully, some magic that attracts good young men into Hunt service, and may that magic continue to work for ever and ever.

10

The Whipper-in

Now we come to the duties of the Whipper-in. How I abominate the expression 'Whip'. To me a 'whip' is something you carry, and for hunting it must have a thong – no cutting whips please – which you crack if you can, but only when it is appropriate to do so. I realise that in practice it is far quicker to shout 'Whip on your right', and perhaps I will concede that the expression may be used in those circumstances; but in general conversation do let the man have his proper title which, after all, is expressly designed to describe his duties.

People tend to dismiss the Whipper-in as a man of little importance, but to my mind he can and should be, so to speak, the Huntsman's right arm. A really good Whipper-in can make all the difference to a Huntsman's life, and a promising young man who obeys orders instantly, but is quick, observant and not afraid of using his own initiative, should go far in good Hunt service.

A Whipper-in's duties vary according to the country, and are very different in a galloping one from those expected of him in rough country, where he may spend most of his time tucked away in dense woodland. In choosing a Whipper-in, it is important to consider the sort of country where he has gained his experience and let that determine which of the candidates you take, should two of them seem to be of similar ability and qualifications.

Again, I hope I am preaching to the converted when I implore Masters to mount their Whippers-in with as much care as they take for themselves or their Huntsman. He is of no use if he cannot get to hounds and stop them if necessary. It is a thoroughly false economy to cut down in this direction, for it is better to have no Whipper-in at all than one so badly mounted that he cannot do his job.

While talking of horses, it is essential to be sure that your Whipper-in understands exactly how much to expect of his horse, and that he realises that it is not a motor-cycle that can go for an unlimited time without tiring. Consideration must always be given to horses, and they should never be taken and galloped in the deepest and worst places where a few yards to right or left there is reasonably hard ground; nor should they be put over the biggest place in a fence when there is a choice. A horse must be nursed at all times, for you never know when a run is going to be fast and far, and it may be impossible to get the second horses up. These remarks, of course, apply to every horse that comes out in the hunting field, and not only those ridden by hunt servants.

Whippers-in are in fact serving a sort of apprenticeship – that such an apprenticeship can go on into middle age is neither here nor there. Most young men worth their salt, when acting as Second Whipper-in are eager to step into the shoes of the First Whipper-in, and their eventual ambition generally is to carry the horn themselves.

In smaller establishments where a special Kennelman is not employed for the care of the hounds, the Whippers-in are responsible for the cleanliness and general well-being of the whole establishment. Their various duties are allocated to them by the Huntsman, but it is likely that the more arduous of these fall to the lot of the Second Whipper-in. In many of the smaller Hunts nowadays, the Whippers-in have to do their own horses, as a Stud-groom with staff under him is an expense that simply cannot be afforded.

Without going into too much detail, the Whippers-in for the most part are responsible for doing the cooking for the pack in the absence of a Kennelman, examining hounds and treating any wounds they may find, watching for and reporting hounds that are at all off-colour, and cleaning and keeping clean the kennels, in particular the lodging rooms and the hounds themselves. Of course, all of this work is done under the direct supervision of the Huntsman, who may in fact prefer to do the actual investigatory and remedial work on his hounds himself.

To give an idea of how the Whipper-in's day goes, when the pack is eventually under way to the Meet the early morning duties having been carried out, the First Whipper-in has to ride ahead and keep a wary eye open for cars on a country road if hounds are hacking on. No hound must pass his horse, and he must try to get car drivers to show consideration and caution – no easy task these days. Behind him comes the Huntsman with his hounds in front of him. The job of the Second Whipper-in is to keep the pack together and to hold back

Giving instructions to my Whipper-in near Easton Grey, the home of Mr and Mrs Peter Saunders

the Field when a hound stops either to empty himself or to vomit. This is a necessary part of the hacking-on and is one of the reasons why hounds are unboxed some way from the Meet.

At the Meet, it is the job of the Whippers-in to help the Huntsman maintain discipline over the pack, ensuring that they remain in a quiet little bunch around the Huntsman's horse. Should one or two break away, they must be fetched back quickly and quietly.

When the signal is eventually given for hounds to move off, the Whippers-in take up the same positions as they did on their way to the Meet, but within half a mile of the covert that is to be drawn the Huntsman will usually stop and send both his Whippers-in on for a view. He himself will walk his horse to the covert side, taking his time and thus giving the men a chance to get into place before a fox can slip out unnoticed and make good his escape.

While hounds are drawing, the Whipper-in's job is to sit as quietly as possible, watching and being ready to help the instant he is required. Should he find hounds rioting, he must endeavour to check them quietly. ' 'Ware heel!' should be said as softly as possible and still be effective and, if he is in a big covert he must not take his eyes off the ride for an instant. If he does, it is almost certain that the fox will choose that very instant to cross. If he does see a fox slip over and holloas, then he must watch the ride even more closely, for the very fact that he has given voice may cause the fox to slink back the way he came.

When sent on down-wind or to the far end of a covert, the Whipper-in must take care not to sit at the exact point of the angle of that covert. He will be quite wrong if he does so, for if a fox does not actually come out at that point, he will probably go there to have a look round to see if it seems safe to do so. Some foxes are so brash that if they want to leave covert then they will do so, not caring a jot who sees them, but these bold spirits are few and far between. However, most determined foxes will break cover eventually, but it has been said that while one small child can prevent a fox coming out, a regiment of cavalry cannot make him go back in. The Whipper-in then should choose a point where he can command as great a view of the country as possible, and yet remain unobserved.

Should two or three of the Field follow the Whipper-in to his viewpoint, there must be no conversation. Although I know how difficult it is for a young and perhaps inexperienced Whipper-in to do so, he should ask these people politely but firmly either to move away a little, or else to sit quietly and help him to watch without either talking or smoking. If they are the right sort, they will not take offence.

When at last the fox does break, then not a sound must be uttered until he has got right away and through at least two, and better still three, fences; even further will not matter. He is unlikely to turn back when he has gone that far and, what is even more important, he is likely then to run straight. That will be far better both for hounds and for those who follow them. A fox that has had a clear start is much more likely to give a good straight run with a point of from five to six miles than one that is running with hounds hard on his brush.

Once the Whipper-in has viewed the fox and has seen it out of sight, then he should holloa three or four times. This is quite enough, for should the Huntsman not hear these holloas, he is not likely to hear any other, and the possibility is that, unbeknown to his

Hound control is most important on main roads. It is a good thing nothing was coming towards us on this corner! (William Morris)

Whipper-in, he may have clapped the main body of the pack on to another fox on the other side of the covert. In that case prolonged holloaing may only have the disastrous effect of dividing the pack. Another important thing is that whenever he does view a fox, a Whipper-in should watch it right out of sight – and so should any-one who wants to be in a position to give constructive help.

While he is waiting for the Huntsman to come up, the Whipper-in should stop any hounds that are hunting the line of the fox out of covert ahead of the main body of the pack, holding them up until the main body arrives. This applies really to fewer than four couple, more than this number being an indication that these are the leading hounds, and therefore that the pack is hunting the line out. If the Huntsman brings the pack to the holloa, the Whipper-in should remain where he has seen the fox, with his cap in his hand pointing in the direction it has gone. As soon as the leading hounds of the pack have settled on to their fox, the Whipper-in who viewed it originally should holloa 'Forrard away, forrard away, forrard!' thus giving the signal to any hounds left in covert and to the other Whipper-in and the Field that the chase has been launched into the open. It is for this signal that the Field should wait before they start galloping – not for the first holloa.

My grandfather did not at all like the idea of a Whipper-in on one side of a covert with the second on the other, the duty of the first being to make his best way to hounds when a fox went away, and the duty of the second being to wait and bring on any hounds that might have been left behind. He quoted Will Long:

> Hounds are like children, they do not like to be left behind, and if they know you will wait, they don't hurry themselves, but they will stop just inside the fence peeping at the huntsman and pack waiting, and will not come on till they see them moving off (this, of course, when there is no fox on foot); or if hounds are away with a fox will try and do a bit of hunting for themselves, in some independent way; and why? because they know that someone will come back and fetch them.

However, times have changed and although perhaps before the war I would have been inclined to agree, nowadays, because of the appalling traffic problems, it is essential that a Whipper-in should collect stray hounds and bring them on.

I firmly believe that the Second Whipper-in should never go on to the next covert or part of a woodland until the whole Hunt is

completely committed to new ground. A sinking fox, or even one
that is just starting to get tired, so often tries to shake off the pursuit
by turning short and going back into covert.

The job of a Whipper-in is to be seen in his right place at all times,
and to be heard as little as possible. If, for instance, he uses his
voice to rate hounds from some distance away, and does not then
immediately go up to them and do something about it, the next time
they hear his voice they will take not a jot of notice. If he has
occasion to use the whip, then he should do so before he administers
a rating, for the moment a hound has been rated down will go his
stern and into the body of the pack he will fly – thus making it
impossible for the Whipper-in to aim accurately. The only voice that
should be heard when leaving a blank covert should be the Huntsman's. If the Whipper-in's voice is constantly heard, it will make
hounds slow in coming when a fox has actually gone. It is only
possible to make a certain volume of noise, and if you do it to the full
all the time how can hounds ever learn to differentiate?

My grandfather said that a Whipper-in whose ambition it is
eventually to become a Huntsman must cherish his voice in private,
and not allow it to be heard too loudly in the hunting field. While a
good voice is obviously a vital asset to a Huntsman, it can be a
positive disadvantage to a Whipper-in.

Another thing that my grandfather observed was that nine out of
ten Whippers-in interfere with hounds when they should not, and
I heartily agree with him. For example: his hounds having checked,
and knowing that he is a long way behind his fox, the Huntsman
will then make his cast. One, two or three couple of hounds with
possibly finer noses than others will go very slowly and perhaps stop
while they puzzle out the scent. On no account at this point should
the Whipper-in interfere with them. Leaving those well alone, he
should put the others on to the Huntsman but at the same time he
must watch closely and, should there be any sign of them
feathering, he must quickly draw the Huntsman's attention to the
fact. It is sad, but true, that some Whippers-in seem to forget that
hounds come out in order to use their noses and to hunt a fox,
and not to be taken abruptly away from their task!

While hounds are running, the duty of the First Whipper-in is to
do everything he can to help his Huntsman, not only by trying to do
the obvious, but also by trying to help him in his constant task of
anticipating future trouble – here he can provide that extra pair of
eyes that the Huntsman so much needs. As second-in-command, he
must ride as close to the Huntsman as possible without either getting

in his way or interfering with hounds. Through the length of a run there will always be wire to cut or pull down, electric wires to be taken up and laid on the ground, gates that cannot be jumped and have either to be wrenched open or even lifted off their hinges if they are padlocked or jammed in any way. It must always be remembered that it should never be necessary for the Huntsman to leave his horse except when he is crossing a piece of boggy ground that must be drawn on foot. This is where members of the Field can help by holding a horse, or giving a hand with a heavy gate. The other members of the Field must always remember that while one of their company remains unmounted after having given this sort of help, on no account must the rest of them move on until he is back on his horse. The only people who are permitted to leave one of the Field in those circumstances are the Master and the hunt servants.

The First Whipper-in has to be prepared to turn his hand to all kinds of tasks: at one moment striking hard blows at an unyielding padlock, and the next riding like a cowboy rounding up stock and urging them well out of the way of a gate that has to be opened. Here again the Field can be helpful by making absolutely certain that nothing escapes. Should such a misfortune befall, all the animals must be put back in their original field, even if it means losing the Hunt altogether. I am sorry, but that is a hunting fact of life.

The Second Whipper-in has quite a different role, for it is he who encourages the tail hounds forward. He counts them constantly, going back to look for the missing ones – a beastly task on a cold, wet winter's evening, when the light is rapidly going and there may be a couple or two missing, with not a scrap of information available as to their whereabouts. It is the Second Whipper-in who has to go on searching when the rest of the hounds are in their hound van on the way home and as for the Field – they are probably enjoying a drink by a roaring fire in the Rose and Crown, or a hot bath and a nice tea at home! The Second Whipper-in deserves a good deal of sympathy and understanding. A quotation from David Brock's *To Hunt the Fox* sums it up admirably:

A whipper-in's task is not one requiring great technical skill. What it does require is a quick brain, an eye for a country, a great deal of common sense, a keen sense of discipline and, perhaps above all, a sense of humour. There is little real enjoyment on a cold December night – especially if you are already wet to the skin, tired, hungry, riding a leg-weary horse of extremely plebeian ancestry, and twelve miles from kennels – to be had out of being

*My cousin and heir, David Somerset, who is also my Joint Master, riding with me
to the Meet*

sent three miles in the wrong direction to search a hilly forest of
some thousand acres for a foxhound which you, personally, think
is an encumbrance to the Pack. If, on your eventual arrival at the
kennels four hours later, you can laugh on being told that 'Lawful
was in by half-past three', you are well on the road to being a
whipper-in.

There are very many pubs in Gloucestershire and in South Wales bearing my name.
This is a particularly good portrait, I think, at Hawksbury

11

In the Field

It is in my capacity as a Master of Hounds for over fifty years, and not from practical experience as a member of the Field, that I feel justified in telling you what I consider to be your duties in the hunting field. I hope the following observations, the result of my many years of experience, may be of use to you, and help you to enjoy your hunting even more.

My grandfather said: '. . . hunting is the amusement, and not the business of a gentleman. He is at perfect liberty, therefore, to pursue it in the way which pleases him and suits him best, provided, of course, *the gratification of his own tastes is compatible with the equal liberties of others.*' Those last italicised words convey in a nutshell what it is I want to say to you. He went on to say: '. . . Of the two classes into which hunting men may be broadly divided, the men who ride to hunt and the men who hunt to ride, it should always be remembered that the *sportsman*, as distinguished from the mere *hunting man*, will be found in the former.' Here again, he conveys my sentiments exactly.

Of course I appreciate that there is a lot to be said for a good gallop, with the added thrill and challenge of crossing unknown country and facing formidable fences on a good horse. I am also well aware that it is necessary to qualify point-to-point horses, and that a day in the hunting field, whether it be a good hunting day or a bad one, is of infinite value in the training of a youngster whether its final destiny is to become a hunter, a steeple-chaser or possibly a potential three-day eventer of international repute. Nobody could deny that.

What I would like to say though is that to me fox-hunting is a truly serious business – and everyone knows this. It therefore follows that those dedicated beings who come out solely for the pleasure of watching hounds working and also to add to what is almost certainly their already considerable knowledge of fox-hunting, are those members of the Field who are dear to my heart. If this book can in any way swell their numbers, then it will have served its purpose.

Although there are very few people nowadays who can claim to know the names of many of the hounds, let alone their pedigrees, there are always a good number who know the line from every covert, the most practicable place in every fence, the ford to every brook, every gate and every byroad in the whole country. With little danger to their own lives or limbs, or those of anybody else, they are therefore in a position to see far more of the day's fun, and will be able to give a far more accurate account at the end of the day of how hounds ran, than those who ride solely for the thrills – and also the spills.

I will finish what I have to say about this with another quotation from Peter Beckford. You must forgive me if you find it a little scathing, but it does sum up what all dedicated foxhunters feel:

> Gentlemen who hunt for the sake of the ride, who are indifferent about the hounds, and know little about the business, if they do no harm, fulfil as much as we have reason to expect from them.

Nearly everyone boxes their horses on to the Meet nowadays, or perhaps employs a second-horseman or girl groom to take them on. Whenever possible I myself have always liked to ride on with hounds, at any rate part of the way. I feel strongly that this is a necessary part of my duties as Master, but I do feel that members of the Field can learn a lot from hacking their own horses on the Meet whenever they can. In the first place, it will get you much fitter than you otherwise could possibly be – especially if your hunting is strictly limited by the amount of time you can spare from your work. It will also enable you to see for yourself that your horse's back is down and it is well settled by the time hounds move off. I find nothing more alarming than starting off fast downhill on a horse that is likely to stage a rodeo act for the benefit of all the onlookers.

There are many things that can be learnt from riding through the country, ranging from the sequence of crops to the names of the farmers through whose land you are riding. There are many points of interest to look for: the condition of the gates perhaps – it may be possible to find out whose responsibility their maintenance is, the tenant farmer's or the landlord's. Why has a hitherto grass field suddenly been ploughed, and why is one side of the road mainly ploughland and the other side grass? Possibly you may find yourself riding along in the company of a local farmer, and there will certainly be many things you can learn from him with regard to the general farming policy of the district. These are the sort of things that will make it much easier for you to understand for instance why the Master decides to draw a covert one way or another – for it is the Master's business to be aware that a particular farmer is anxious to keep the Hunt out of certain fields from time to time for varying reasons. These reasons will by no means necessarily indicate an anti-hunting feeling, but will more likely be signs of good husbandry.

People are very fond of saying that farmers are always grumbling about something, and that they are never satisfied either with the weather or with prices. I think it is a good idea for members of a Hunt to try to understand the reasons behind this so-called 'grumbling', so that they can form their own opinion as to whether the farmers are in fact justified in their complaints.

Farming is undoubtedly the backbone of our country and the Hunts certainly could not exist without the goodwill of the farmers, and not just their goodwill but their active help and participation too. One of my few regrets – and I must say I do not have many – is that I myself never studied agriculture seriously, even if only for six months.

Whatever happens, you must not be late for the Meet. That may sound like unnecessary advice, but unfortunately it is not. I find it a great nuisance having latecomers arriving from all sides, and I also think unpunctuality is extremely bad manners. 'Punctuality is the politeness of Princes' is by no means an idle saying for, when examined, it goes much deeper than is immediately obvious. I have found that people who are not punctual are likely to be unreliable in many other ways; and unreliability in the hunting field is a serious fault.

I do not like people to unbox their horses too close to the Meet for it causes unnecessary congestion on what are already over-full roads. It can also be dangerous, as there are always many people about on their feet in the vicinity of a Meet of hounds. My Field are requested to unbox at least half a mile away. In any case, as I said earlier, it is much better for your horse, and for you, to have a hack.

(overleaf) My hounds drawing a field of roots in April (hence my rat-catcher's garb)

Try always to give yourself plenty of time so that you are not tempted to trot on as soon as you mount, for that is very bad for your horse, and can lead to all kinds of health troubles.

Should you need to cross country on your way to the Meet, whatever you do avoid coverts and if, by an unavoidable accident, you find that you are going to be late for the Meet, then ride the roads until you can join hounds. In that way you will run no risk of disturbing an edgy fox, or even of heading it.

I always advertise my Meets as being at 10.45am, and that means that we move off on the dot of 11am. This ensures that we get a prompt start to the day's hunting, which is especially valuable at the end of the year, when it is not possible to draw again much after 3pm.

There are two cardinal rules that should be followed when riding to hounds. The first is that you must use your own judgement whenever possible, and so you must know what to do, where to go and more or less what is happening, so that you are capable of making up your mind quickly, instantly weighing up the pros and cons of any particular course of action, and then proceeding without hesitation.

The second is that you must try to keep cool. It is not the slightest use getting excited or flustered out hunting, for all it will do is upset your horse as well as yourself, and then you will find that everything is going wrong. In my experience, when you hear people being badly cross, the chances are that they are frightened. People who are either frightened of their horses or of the hazards they imagine they are going to have to face, often react by being angry with something or somebody else – seldom with themselves. This of course is human nature and does not apply only to the hunting field, for when people are worried they often get angry, and it is their nearest and dearest who are most likely to suffer from their wrath.

The third thing about which I would like to speak, but which can hardly come under the heading of a 'cardinal rule', is nerve and courage. I cannot say that I thought very much about the subject until I cast aside the gay abandon of early youth and began to think of the consequences of hard falls on ageing bones.

It is evident that there are some people who do not seem to know what fear is. I think it is possible that they may lack imagination, and in that case I feel sorry for them, for without that quality life must be a dull business. On the other hand it may well be that they are very clever at hiding their true feelings, but this is not a subject on which I would like to be called to make a judgement. There are some people who are simply foolhardy and over-confident, and this leads them to take needless risks, not only endangering themselves but possibly causing others to have accidents too.

Courage readily divides into two categories: the moral and the purely physical. I believe that the truly courageous man – and in the present context this means the one who rides straight to hounds – will have a certain amount of both in his make-up. A little moral courage which will enable him to confess his weakness, even if only to himself, must be a good thing for anybody to possess. True courage is the courage of judgement; for the man who can weigh up the risks and still go ahead in the face of adversity must be truly courageous.

In fact, to refer to someone as 'brave out hunting' is not really correct, for although there is no doubt that a really good rider to hounds is courageous, he cannot really be described as brave. Being brave means doing something, not because you want to, but because you feel you should. There is no doubt at all that the first-flighters adore their hunting, one of the reasons they go so well is because they are doing the thing they love doing best in the world.

There is little doubt that people will do things when they are hunting that they would never consider in cold blood. It is almost as if they have had a shot of some sort of drug that dulls their normal fears – for who would think of jumping an iron gate for the fun of it except perhaps the very young or, may I be permitted to say, the foolhardy? It always amazes me to see the eventers and show jumpers taking on the massive fences that they do without the sound of hounds in front to stir their blood. That to me spells real courage, though I am told by modest competitors of this sort that it is the very fact that they are competing that injects the necessary adrenalin into the system.

So with judgement to help you to make up your mind what should be done, coolness to help you to carry out the actions and, finally, the nerve to help you to throw your heart over the obstacle in front, you should be set to take on all kinds of countries. And the very best of luck to you and, more important still, good hunting!

To begin with, when hounds move off from the Meet you must try to get a good place reasonably near to them on the way to the first draw. You never know your luck, for a fox may jump out of a hedge, and the nearer you are to the scene of action the better. On your arrival at the covert side, take a good look round and make a few mental notes. Study the general lie of the land and make sure that you know which way the wind is really blowing, taking no notice of the sudden little eddies and swells that always occur round corners. It is a help to try to put yourself in the fox's place and decide where you yourself would break cover in the conditions that prevail. Work out a quick getaway in the light of your conclusions, but have alternative plans ready just in case your guesswork is wrong.

Once at the covert side, I think you should be prepared to follow the fortunes of the pack to the bitter end. I do not hold with people who bring their horses out 'just for an hour to see hounds'. Better for them to go for a long ride instead.

If the Field are chattering like a lot of starlings, try to draw away a little so that you can hear the Huntsman's voice, but whatever you do never follow him or ride in his track. This maxim always holds good, as there is nothing more maddening for a Huntsman than to have members of the Field dogging his footsteps. And do remember, if you have a professional Huntsman, the words of R. S. Summerhays:

> A privilege vested in all Masters who hunt their own hounds is to swear at their field as loud and as long as they wish, and although this is much criticised in these modern days, the use of this safety valve is denied to the professional huntsman.

The Huntsman needs to be alone so that he can use his ears properly. It is quite likely that the squelching approach of another horse, with its attendant jingling, may just prevent him from hearing the first hound open as a fox is unkennelled.

Again always bear in mind that the nearer you are to the scene of action at the outset, the more likely you are to maintain a good place later on. One of the secrets of getting a good start, and you must remember that everyone has an equal chance, is to be on the alert. So many people never learn – they chatter away, smoke and sit idly about on their horses, keeping their eyes and ears figuratively speaking shut, letting their horses become unbalanced, with the result that when the Field Master finally lets them go they are simply not attending, and therefore must get off to a bad start.

You will undoubtedly find that you will have a distinct advantage by taking your own line, and that is not entirely a matter of courage. Quite apart from the fact that you will have time to use your own judgement as to where to take the next fence without being hampered by other horses or influenced by where the chap in front of you has jumped, your horse will certainly go better out in front. He will have nothing to distract his attention, and is therefore not going to be made careless in an effort to pass the horse in front of him. It is when he is tearing along, either trying to keep or to catch up, that he will make mistakes. Remember too that hunt staff seldom fall, and this undoubtedly is because they are out in front. So if you yourself are out in front, you are likely to have a more confident, safe and therefore enjoyable ride than if you find yourself having to queue at the end of a big Field – perhaps waiting for a hundred or more people to negotiate four or five narrow fences ahead, with all the attendant refusals and tumbles. When this happens you will thereafter always be 'running' even to keep up with the walking pace that is all that hounds in front are perhaps maintaining.

Should you find that you have missed your place at the first gate, move down the road about twenty-five yards and pop over the fence as inconspicuously as possible, distracting your horse's attention from the crowd by using your rein and heel on the farthest side away from the gate. Nothing can be more ignominious when attempting what the critics might call a slightly theatrical start, than to have your horse refuse and tip you into the ditch. And if you do go some distance away, should he then refuse, at any rate you will not bump into the crowd that will still be surging round the gate.

When you are away with a good start, you must try to take a line about fifty to a hundred yards to the right or left of the pack, always remembering where the wind is, and therefore keeping on the down-wind side. Whatever happens, you must not ride a line between the Huntsman and his hounds as long as he is well up to them. If however he is tailing them, which is unlikely at the outset of a run, then you are at liberty to take up your position at the side without any risk of getting in the way or of being sworn at.

Riding fast and straight to hounds is a gift, and out of a Field of say 150, you are rarely going to find more than about five and twenty people who will remain in the first flight the whole day. Generally speaking, of course, these people will be extremely well mounted. But I would like to wager – if I were a betting man which I am not! – that should they all change horses with the next five and twenty coming along behind in the second flight, then it would be exactly the same group of people who would immediately surge ahead again. They possess a certain gift, a *je ne sais quoi*, of always being in the front when hounds are running. Basically it must have a lot to do with courage and good horsemanship, but more than anything it must be due to that eye for the country that is an essential part of successful riding to hounds.

An eye for country is something that you either have or have not, though I daresay it is possible to develop it to some extent as you gain more and more experience. A strong bump of locality, a general awareness of the surroundings, and the full use of all the faculties of observation, will all play a part in helping the would-be fox-hunter to acquire this very desirable quality. It may be that it ought to be described as a qualification, for it is certainly a very necessary adjunct of really successful riding to hounds.

If it is a good scenting day, you can hope to have a wonderful time. Once you are away to a good start and you have got yourself a good place, you will be able to assess the state of the scent. If it is good, you must ride your horse in the words of an amateur Huntsman of fifty years ago who was renowned for always being in the same Field as his hounds: 'up to 75 per cent of his value'.

David Brock said in his admirable book *The Fox-hunter's Week-end Book*, published just before the last war:

> Ride the first four fields of every hunt as though hounds were about to run one hundred miles straight on end in little under 60 minutes; then you will get your place, and if they really do run, you will not have to make up lost ground. On the other hand, if it is one of those 'rotten bad scenting days' you can, as soon as you discover that fact, pull up, and take the easiest line.

I would like to add a word or two of my own to this and say that before going off like a bat out of hell, you must make absolutely certain that hounds really have a proper line. The early hotting up of horses unnecessarily is to be avoided at all costs, and I find that far too often some riders will gallop across a couple of fields to the first covert before hounds have been put in to draw. This can do nothing but harm because not only does it make their own horses unduly excited but it disturbs many others. Although naturally I agree and indeed advocate that you must try to make a good 'get away', you must still ride with wisdom and caution. The one thing you cannot do is to pass the Huntsman and the pack – at any rate, not if you want to go out with the same Hunt again! So when you have covered your first four fields, thus making sure of your place, put your horse into a nice easy gallop and keep him like that so that, when it is necessary for him to exert himself for a succession of jumps, he will still have that extra bit to get him over.

Do not forget that however long a run may seem to be, in reality hounds very seldom run for more than twenty minutes at a time without a check, or at any rate without a short breathing space. As long as you are well up with them, you will be able to take full benefit of that breather. Turn your horse's head to the wind for a moment or two so that he can catch his breath before the next burst, but while you are doing so you must not forget to keep an eye on hounds, and try to mark the one that is the first to open again on the line.

On a bad scenting day, a piece of wise advice is to keep well away from the Huntsman and the Master, for tempers are bound to be frayed. You know that the worse the scent, the slower hounds will hunt. Therefore they will be further and further away from their fox all the time, unless it is taking a rest or has dropped dead in its stride. I really believe there are some people who honestly think that hounds will run that much faster after every check on a bad scenting day. I suppose one ought to admire them for their zeal and optimism, but I do wish they would try to learn from experience, as they undoubtedly provide yet another of the crosses that have to be borne by Master and Huntsman on such evil days. In fact, on those miserable days it is wiser to keep to the gates, thus saving your horse – and incidentally the fences – for another and a better day. It may mean that you go fifty per cent further, but you will neither be tiring your horse nor exasperating a long-suffering farmer by jumping and encouraging others behind you to jump his fences. In fact this may be one of the times when you would be justified in going home, saving your horse for another and perhaps better day.

There are, alas, people who will always ride on the tail of hounds. There is no doubt at all that hounds tend to take their sense of direction to a greater or lesser degree from the horses that are following them, but there are not many people who realise this. It follows that it is only too easy to press them past the spot where perhaps, the fox jinked and then, if it is a bad scenting day, the sport is likely to be over. Luckily on good scenting days things are quite different, for hounds will be tearing along in any case far ahead of the horses and then those people who will not learn can do no harm.

Should you view a fox, turn your horse's head in the direction you saw it travelling and stand up in your stirrups, taking off your hat and pointing with it in the same direction (therefore no hatstring please). In Moorland countries it is customary to wave a white handkerchief which shows up better against the background, and this is a necessary part of hunting equipment in those parts.

As you stand up in your stirrups, cast a glance at your watch, and if the Huntsman is out of sight, then you may holloa. If the Huntsman comes to your holloa, you must tell him accurately what you know, and leave him to judge for himself if what you saw was the hunted fox or not. If possible, describe the fox, tell him how fast it was travelling, and try to indicate with absolute certainty the place where it went, having of course watched it out of sight so that you have pinpointed exactly where it slipped over a fence. Mark that place in your mind by a particular tree or bush, so that you can say with assurance that it went so far to the right or to the left of it at exactly such and such a time. It is then up to the Huntsman to take the appropriate action, but you will know that you have done your bit.

I am reminded here of a piece from *Young Tom Hall* by R. S. Surtees:

Having looked the people saucily over, and given himself as many airs as he could, Dicky looked at his gold watch, and, seeing it only wanted five and twenty minutes to twelve, he shut it against his cheek, and, drawing on his red-lined dog-skin gloves, took his grey horse short by the head, and, rising in his stirrups, proceeded to address the throng, for Field we can hardly call them. 'Now gen'l'men,' said he, looking around him, 'as my lord's away, the conduct of affairs naturally devolves upon me, and I'll take it as a 'tickler favour if you'll all come into cover, and keep there, and refrain from holloaing. It's been well observed,' continued he, 'that every man sees the hunted fox; but as we only undertake to pursue one at a time with our hounds – which, I may observe, are bred with the greatest care and attention, containing strains of almost every fashionable blood – the Belvoir, the Burton, the Beaufort, the Quorn, to say nothing of a dash of the old Pytchley Furrier – I say, as we only undertake to pursue one fox at a time, you'll p'r'aps have the goodness to let the hounds select their own!'

Another way in which you may find yourself able to help a hard-pressed Huntsman is by getting into the habit of counting hounds whenever possible, especially when they are going through a gap or a gate and you find yourself standing nearby, or if you see some on the skyline going out of sight. You never know when such information may be of the greatest use to him and, if you get a reputation for accuracy, he will recognise you as a useful member of the Field.

Should you by any ill-chance find yourself getting behind, you are going to have to make double use of all your senses, specially your eyes. Watch the leading horses even if hounds themselves are out of sight and earshot, and when they swing, swing with them;

but you must take the chord of the circle rather than the arc, thus enabling yourself to cut corners.

If you are keeping down-wind of the pack as you should be, if they turn it will be to you, and if they have gone down into a dip you should be able to hear them. You must get into the habit of looking for signs, just as the hunt servants do. For instance, when you are in sheep country, you must throw your eyes forward, not only to see where you are going but to see if sheep are huddled together on a distant hillside. If they are you may be sure that they are not there to keep warm. In all probability they have seen or heard something that has frightened or disturbed them, and has made them crowd together for the comfort that sheep seem to get from close contact with their own kind. More likely than not they have seen or heard hounds, as sheep often take little notice of a fox loping through their midst.

Once you have reached the top of a hill, do not move for a minute or two, watch and listen and go on only when you are sure that hounds have gone right down to the bottom and there is little chance of them returning. There is no point in wearing your horse out by galloping it unnecessarily up hills. Remember too when crossing hills that it is better to go round the rim than over the top, again to spare your horse.

Now for a word of caution. Pay little attention to holloas – a blast on a whistle is a different thing, for that will have been blown by a member of the hunt staff – and always follow the golden rule of waiting to see what hounds do before acting yourself. This rule applies, perhaps even more so, if you have seen what you think is the hunted fox, and may even have given voice yourself. Nothing can be worse than to gallop off for several fields only to find that there is no sign of a hound and, when you return, you see them streaming up a distant hillside in the opposite direction. It hardly seems necessary to remind you that it is the hounds that are hunting the fox and not you! Believe me, though, in the heat of the moment, and especially when people are inexperienced, this is something that is only too easily forgotten.

I would now like to give some advice to those who are either new to the hunting field or to a particular country. First I suggest you pick a pilot. To do this, you must try to choose one of the knowledgeable people always to be found in every Hunt. If you are in a strange country, you will probably have already had a word with the Secretary before coming, and he will certainly be able to give you sound advice about this. These knowledgeable people are quite easy to spot. You will generally find them standing quietly, probably not gossiping over-much, at the Meet, and looking carefully at the hounds. I would often place my money on a good farmer as a pilot, but never make the mistake of thinking that because a man is not in the first flush of youth he is not going to ride both straight and fast!

If you are going to follow a pilot, whatever happens he must be given plenty of room. Should he show a marked distaste for being followed – and there are many people who really hate it – you must find somebody else. If you keep at fifty yards' distance, you will be able to see what your leader is doing without being too conspicuous or riding obviously 'in his pocket'. This is a difficult thing to do in a large and crowded Field, but it is the best procedure.

I cannot emphasise too much that in a strange country it is a great mistake to try to take your own line, even along the roads, unless you happen to be one of those men who are born with such a good eye to a country that it almost makes them appear to be minor prophets. Indeed, this instinct is so highly developed among a few people that should they be dropped by helicopter into the middle of the Field in any Hunt where hounds were running hard, I swear they would soon find the best and quickest way to the end of the hunt.

Many a good hunt has been spoilt by the man who, when trying to catch up, has unknowingly headed the fox. Should you find yourself in the unenviable position of being on your own in entirely strange country, then the old tenets must be well in the forefront of your mind: keep well down-wind, your eyes open and in front of you and, most important of all, listen carefully. By so doing, you may even be in a position to produce some valuable information at a crucial moment.

Wherever you are, should you find yourself in trouble with either the Master or the Field Master you must never argue or answer back. Keep quiet and remember that in these particular circumstances, more perhaps than at any other time, silence certainly is golden. You will probably have an opportunity to explain your actions later on, away from the heat of the moment, and you will find that your explanation will then be more readily received. Do not forget the old French saying: *qui s'excuse, s'accuse*; in other words, the more excuses you make, the more you are liable to damn yourself.

There is no doubt that it is impossible to hunt without expecting (anticipating would be too strong a term) falls. If you are out with hounds and want to be in a position to see what they are doing,

Members of the Grafton Hunt demonstrating the need for care in crowded gateways
(Frank H. Meads)

you must be prepared to take a toss or two. But the more responsible a man is, the less likely he is to risk his neck. Equally, the more falls he has had, the more chary he will become about having more.

Your first care should be to take your fences at the same time as your horse – together, not separately, as Assheton Smith so aptly put it. A good rule is to try never to part company with your horse until the last possible moment. Then, if the parting seems inevitable, try to keep hold of your reins. (Do not, though, hang on to them if it is at all likely that by so doing you will be dragged.) Staying on your horse is an art that you are obliged to learn if you do a stint in the mounted section of the Army, for there it is a punishable offence to dismount before you are given the command!

Some people have strong views that a rider maintains his seat either by balance or by grip. I think it is maintained by a mixture of both – by grip from the seat down and by balance from the hips up. This co-ordination of effort is comparable with the musician's use of hands and ear or mouth. So above the waist the body should be light and supple, ready to give and take with every movement of the horse. From the hips down it should be as strong and unyielding as iron. The correct position in the dead centre of the horse's back is illustrated in pictures of the ancient Greeks who rode their horses without the benefit of saddles, and it is the position that gives the greatest comfort to horse and rider. Never forget that horses can sum up the abilities of their riders much more quickly than any human being – and just as fast will see to it that they part company.

When taking fences, the first lesson to be learnt is what George Walters taught me when I was twelve years old – lean forward. It is not quite as simple as that, but there are plenty of experts to whom you can go for advice and tuition if you wish. What I can tell you can only be from my own experience in the hunting field – and jumping has become such a professional business over the last couple of decades. There are many fine horsemen and women about nowadays, but it is not enough to be an experienced and courageous cross-country rider to qualify as a successful rider to hounds. This book is intended to help you to hunt, not to event or to show jump, so I hope that what I have to say will be of use to you in the hunting field.

A primary lesson that is often learnt on the nursery rocking-horse is that balance must be retained while the horse is in the air. The legs from the knee down should go slightly back for, if they are stuck forward so that the whole leg is in a straight line, the shock when the horse lands, especially over a drop fence or on to hard ground, will be so harsh that even if the rider does not have a crashing fall, he may well find himself in serious difficulties.

Never, never hold the cantle or back of the saddle when jumping. A friend of mine saw somebody killed by doing this, for her body twisted and she was not able to save herself. If you feel you must hold on to something, grab the pummel, the martingale, or even a bit of mane, but never hold on behind. If however you are cantering down really precipitous places and find yourself being bounced by the horse's action higher and higher, it is then permissible to hold on behind, as by doing so you will be able to pull yourself down into the right position again.

It is essential to know how to approach fences in the hunting field. You must not expect the horse to do all the work for you, for however experienced a hunter he may be he will still need to be ridden at his fences. What I mean is that his stride should be contracted about twenty yards from the fence by taking hold of his head, and his hocks brought beneath him by use of leg and heel, so that he is collected on reaching the point in the fence where you have decided he should take off. By pulling him together and slowing him down in this way you also give him a little breathing space, and provide him with the opportunity to fill his lungs with air. This rule of collection applies equally both to bold horses and to slugs. If you think it likely that he will refuse, give him a touch of the spurs in good time, thus making up his mind for him. Save your whip on a horse you think is likely to refuse until he has actually jumped in a sloppy way, then bring it down the instant he lands. You will be surprised what an effect it will have at the next jump. This piece of advice was given by a great man who was renowned last century for being always at the front, and it is advice that still holds good today.

The safest jump of all is timber, although it is often the sort of jump that frightens the newcomer to Vale country. But horses can see it, it is solid and often, what is more important, the horse cannot see too much through or beyond it. The very strength of its structure is intended to keep stock in their right places, so it rarely needs any wire, and there is seldom a ditch.

You will find that the more the country over which you are riding slopes downwards, the more likely are the jumps to get bigger and bigger – a feature of Vale country particularly. However it is said, and with a lot of truth, that the big falls are taken by the people who by choice jump the little fences: and I have found that many of the worst injuries are sustained from falls on the flat.

If you are a novice, go slowly. By that, I do not mean hold your horse on a tight rein and walk up to an obstacle and poke his nose over it! We are indebted to television for showing us how the great show jumpers can take the largest fence from a collected canter, or even from a trot, and that is the example we should try to emulate. Most horses can spread themselves to a remarkable extent even from a standstill, and it is always possible to gallop on and make up ground between fences.

There are several good reasons for giving this advice to go slowly. Firstly, your horse will be more collected, and therefore able to use his muscles more effectively for jumping. If your horse does make a mistake then, if you are going fairly slowly, you will be in a better position to sit tight and help him to recover himself. If you are galloping flat out, the chances are that a slight mistake on the part of your mount will catapult you out of the saddle. Secondly, a very good reason for going on the slow side is that you thus enable your horse to look where he is going. Finally, should your horse come down it should not be such a bad fall, and with any luck you will not be hurt yourself and will keep hold of him. Of course, there are exceptions to the rule, and it is possible to go too slowly and find yourself in a big ditch with the horse on top of you.

On the subject of big ditches, if you are not sure whether or not one lurks on the other side of an obstacle, take a quick look at those you know are invariably in front with the hounds. If you see them steadying and collecting their horses some distance away from the obstacle, this is the clue you need. Once you have collected your horse and 'put him right' then leave him alone, and do not interfere with his mouth for the last few strides before he takes off.

One thing you must remember, and which should give you comfort, is that your horse does not want to fall and will therefore do all in his power to save himself, and you. When there is a ditch on the nearside with a fence on the bank, then again you must not go too fast. When you know that a ditch lies on the other side of a bank, you must really go at it. When talking of the way to approach a fence remember that, as in human athletics, a high jump should be approached slowly and a wide jump as fast as possible.

As you approach a fence you will have to ask yourself quickly, 'Is it sound?' and 'Is it level?' If it is not level, then which way does it slope? If the going is sound, you can then make your approach at the pace that seems to you to be the best, but if the take-off is badly poached you must make doubly sure that your horse is collected and has his hocks well under him in order to let him be able to get himself out of the deep and over the jump.

Ground sloping towards the jump presents an additional hazard for, if you go too fast, your horse will tend to slide into it. You must come up to it quietly and then, if he is at all handy, it is best to leave it to your horse. When there is an uphill slope, you will need to speed up to give your horse a chance to spread himself: but beware of going too fast in case he becomes uncollected and his legs slip from under him.

12

Riding to Hounds

A famous Leicestershire man to hounds said that the proper pace for a nice fly fence with a fair ditch on the far side is 'a little faster than a canter'. A fence with a ditch blind to you needs something a bit slower than a canter, and the horse often has the best chance when faced with a big bank that is topped with a trappy fence if he is trotted up to it.

When someone has jumped a place successfully right in front of you, it takes strength of mind as well as muscle power to use your own judgement and jump a little to the left or right, if you really feel it would be better so. Your horse will obviously be getting more and more excited with each approaching fence, and when all is said and done, it is much easier to follow in someone else's footsteps, even though it may not always be the wisest course.

You must get into the habit of looking at the ground in front of a distant fence as well as at the fence itself. You may see what appears to be a weak straggly one, full of holes with no visible wire, but if the ground about it is not poached, you may be sure that there is wire about, for otherwise there would be traces of cattle having gone through. Conversely, if you see a solid-looking fence that appears to be without a gap, yet right in the middle of it the ground is all broken up, you may be equally sure that either there is a gate or a negotiable gap right there. You must always remember that farmers will not waste time, money or labour on wiring good solid fences, nor on those that lie between ploughed fields, for wire is used to control cattle and sheep.

Trappy places need handy horses, and when you are faced with a sheer slide down and a tree plumb in the middle at the bottom, followed immediately by a rocky upward precipice, that is when

An example of riders crowding each other (Frank H. Meads)

your horse should be left alone to look after himself and you. Adopt as firm a seat as you can below the waist, but be ready to twist and duck suddenly if faced with an unexpected sapling or branch.

When following other horses over a jump that necessitates a right-angled turn on landing – it may be that you are jumping into a field that has been sown and will therefore need to go round the edge – make sure that your horse is attending to what he is doing and does not have his eyes on the horses going on in front for that will make him careless.

Take care not to gallop too fast down a ride in a wood, as hounds puzzling out a line will take not the slightest notice of horses, and are liable to race out across the ride just as you go past. If they come out under your horse's feet the consequences could be disastrous. Nearly all rides have intersections at right-angles, and when the horse in front of you turns sharply and unexpectedly, yours will turn too, regardless of how fast he is going. It is very humiliating (not to say painful) to continue up a ride without your

This is the sort of place where it is best to leave it all to the horse and sit as tight as you can: Mr Munro-Wilson hunting with the Tivy-side (Frank H. Meads)

horse! Even if you do stay with the horse, the going is often slippery, and both of you may come down. So be cautious when in covert.

On downland or Moorland country, you can gallop happily along the tracks with impunity. It is when you start to cross these tracks that you can meet all kinds of hazards such as ditches, rabbit holes and unexpected banks, which at first will be totally invisible, both to you and to your horse. Your horse will, however, see them before you do, so you must sit very tight.

If you are a novice, then be a wise novice and determine from the outset to learn as much as you can from watching people with a reputation for crossing country wisely and cautiously, though they may not be among the 'first flighters'. There will be time enough for going faster when you have gained experience. You must never be too proud to learn, either about the art and skill of riding to hounds or, more important still, about the art of hunting the fox.

Always try to spare your horse as much as possible, in the same way that hunt servants have to try to spare theirs. Jump a small place for preference and trot rather than canter. This is most important when you are on a road, for nothing is worse or more jarring for a horse's legs than galloping on tarmac and horses also find it very tiring at the end of a long day being made to gallop along the uneven edge of a road, as it puts them out of balance and can cause a good deal of strain. That is when you must use your discretion, and let them choose the road if they prefer it, if it is safe to do so. If you are young and agile and can remount swiftly and easily, get off when there is a check and save your horse's back.

When ploughed fields are wet, choose the furrow where the water is lying, for that means it has a solid bottom. Rushes indicate wet ground, and you should take a ridge and furrow at a slant. Experience will tell you which grass fields – alas only too conspicuous by their absence in many parts of the land nowadays – can be galloped over with impunity having already been eaten out, and not therefore at their prime waiting for a prize herd to be put there.

When you come to a stream, try to cross where hounds have gone, for they after all follow the fox, and you may be sure that he will have gone over at the narrowest and safest point. If you have not seen hounds cross, and there is no one to follow, you will find that the bank will be firmest where there is a tree or bush. Use that as a take-off if you cannot find a ford, but remember that you must always ride fairly hard at water, or you risk a refusal and a wetting. Go round rather than risk a fall, unless you know your horse is used to jumping water, for the fall could be a bad one.

Mrs Lloyd Mostyn, former Joint Master of the Bicester and Warden Hill Hunt, showing the way to some young followers (Frank H. Meads)

In some hunts it is customary to have gate-closers appointed each day, drawn from a band of volunteers. The South Dorset Hunt (Frank H. Meads)

Above all, never allow yourself to forget what you owe to your horse! At the end of the day try to resist all blandishments of prolonged hospitality and be firm about getting your horse home to his own stable as soon as possible. All horse-masters will bear me out in saying that it is the amount of time that a horse is out of his own box that tells on him, and not necessarily the length or speed of a run. Your own creature comforts can come later.

If you do have to go into a house for any reason, make sure that your horse is warm; try to borrow a rug or blanket to put over his loins, and ask if he can have a very short chilled drink, or even give him some gruel if it is offered. Be as quick as you can – ten minutes, just time for a quick cup of tea or something stronger, is enough. In the olden days, people used to stop at wayside inns on the way home to give their horses gruel mixed with a tankard of ale, but doubtless this practice was as much for their own benefit as for the horse's!

If you have a long hack to your home or to your transport, then a steady jog is the most comfortable pace for your horse, even though it may shake you up a bit; and it does him a world of good if you can get off and walk by his side for a few hundred yards. That will help you too, even though you may not think so at the time!

It is very important to let him walk the last mile or two so that he will arrive cool. When you do get to your transport, rug him up well, using an anti-sweat sheet under his travelling rug, and give him a hay-net to occupy him during the journey, for he will undoubtedly be as hungry as you are. If you use a trailer, close the top if you are in any doubt about draughts, and then it is time to make for home as quickly as you safely can.

Trotting homeward in Spring on the hope we rely
That we reach it ere dark with our hunting-coat dry;
The horse undistress'd by the work he has done,
The rider well pleased with his place in the run.

R. E. Egerton Warburton

13
Fox Coverts and Their Care (with Thoughts on Wire)

No hunting country will provide its full measure of sport unless the fox coverts are maintained in good order. This is another of the many responsibilities of the Master of Hounds, but one he may well decide to depute to others, though I think it is always wise for him to keep a personal eye on the way the work is carried out.

As soon as a covert becomes hollow, a fox will take to lying out, and it is these foxes who are in the main responsible for the claims of poultry-keepers and others. The fox that lies out is a nuisance in many ways, for he will very likely have the tiresome habit of jumping up just at the wrong moment, perhaps cause the attention of hounds to be diverted at a crucial moment in a hunt, and thus to change foxes.

Hazel grows of its own accord in a covert, and presents problems as unless it is cut back regularly it kills all other growth. In the old days when labour was cheap and plentiful it used to be cut in rotation, but now this is impossible, and it grows up higher and higher, leaving the ground hollow underneath. The only answer is to cut and lay it, and even this is becoming a dying art.

The acknowledged expert on fox coverts and their care was Mr Willie Wroughton who lived many years ago and wrote a little book which alas has long been out of print called *The Management of Fox Coverts*, which is well worth reading if you can get hold of a copy. Much of what it contains still holds good – in the way of so much country lore.

A fox covert can never be too thick, and the majority of those in the Midlands consist of blackthorn, gorse or privet. A blackthorn covert, if properly looked after, should hold well for ten years or more as long as the tops are lopped from time to time but, after that, it will have to be cut down and recreated. The best way of getting this work done is to ask a local farmer to undertake it. It is important not to split the stubs with an axe, but to cut through them with an upward stroke. It is a waste of time to cut elder, as it grows again so quickly. It needs to be 'stocked up' by the roots, and then the bare places can be replanted with privet, which is hardy and is generally left alone by rabbits. The waste matter from such a blackthorn covert is sometimes used by farmers for mending fences, but what remains will have to be burnt. The bonfires should be kept small and scattered. After a year, the tops of the tall plants should be slashed with a billhook about three feet from the ground and then again the following year as this will promote a thicker growth below, which in turn will prolong the life of the covert.

When it is necessary to cut a ride through a covert for the Huntsman, it is best to do this in a zig-zag fashion to foil would-be poachers with guns.

The fence or hedge around a covert must be kept in good order, for if it is allowed to grow too high, it will shut out the sun and light. It is a good idea to keep a padlock on the gate during the summer to discourage trespassers.

Gorse coverts have to be cut every half dozen years or so. If the plants are worn out, they should be cut close to the ground, but if not they can be cut off to about eighteen inches and left to sprout. It is very important to ensure that the ground is kept clean after cutting so that the new young growth is not choked by grass or weeds, and it is also imperative that rabbits should be killed and their holes dug in. When the job is finished it should look rather like a well kept garden, all the rubbish having been burnt and the ground as clean as a whistle. By June the seedling gorse should be three or four inches high, and then it can be left to fend for itself. Before that, the young gorse will have to be protected by four-foot high wire netting, eight inches of which should be dug in. Great care must be taken when mounting this operation not to net the rabbits in instead of keeping them out! This wire netting should be left in place for at least eighteen months. Moorland gorse is burnt in March every few years.

Evergreen privet fox coverts when they become hollow and cease to hold properly should be cut close to the ground, fresh plants being put in to replace those that have died. Lonicera, an evergreen, is a very useful plant as it does not grow high like gorse and thorn, but when it has reached about three feet it spreads, and the longer it is left the thicker it grows. The method of planting this useful ever-

Wire is a hazard for hounds (R. Clapperton)

Although the Duke of Buccleuch has had plain wire put in as the top strand of this fence, these hounds are still reluctant to go in to draw the banks of the River Tweed (R. Clapperton)

green is similar to that of gorse – it must be raised in almost garden-like conditions and kept constantly weeded during the first year. Whitethorn and the wild plum are to be found in many well known coverts, but I do not altogether recommend them when you are replanting. If they are already there, the best way to deal with them is to 'layer' them just high enough from the ground to enable a hound to move about underneath. The disadvantage of 'layering' coverts is that when they are beaten down by the weather, particularly by snow, a solid shelf is liable to be formed on which a fox can lie in safety, while hounds draw the covert below. As foxes dislike damp, the greatest care must be taken to drain coverts by means of deep open dykes that will carry off the water.

Barbed wire is a horrible thing, and we fox-hunters may be forgiven if we believe it to be the invention of the devil. However it serves its purpose I suppose, as not only is it the cheapest form of fencing, but it is by far the most effective in preventing heavy stock from damaging fences. Often it is the only alternative to posts and rails in a country where fences will not grow – and posts and rails as we know only too well are prohibitively expensive nowadays, and therefore can really only be considered for high-class bloodstock.

Most hunting countries have now organised themselves into districts, with wire-workers operating in each one.

The job of wire-workers is to try to get all possible wire down before the season starts, while at the same time offering the farmers concerned some acceptable alternative. Where the wire cannot be removed – where there is a registered dairy herd for instance, all of which are required by the Ministry of Agriculture to be fenced by barbed wire – a system of hunt jumps, slip-rails, gates and bridges has to be put up where it is needed. Where wire has to remain it is a good idea to have it well flagged.

Wire-workers also have to see that all damaged fences and gates are repaired as quickly as possible. If they are not then, believe me, up goes the wire, and with justification. It is also their duty at the end of the season to see that all the wire that was removed in the autumn is put back again.

As with so many voluntary workers for the Hunt, their reward lies in the knowledge that they are helping to promote good sport.

14
Earth-stopping

The principles of earth-stopping are simple. Where hounds are going to draw, the earths where the fox is likely to run should have been 'stopped out' or blocked the evening before, after the fox has gone on his nightly prowl and before he returns the next morning to sleep. In the places where foxes are likely to run, the earths should be 'put to' or stopped in the early morning, just in time to prevent the fox going to ground as soon as he has been found. This does not always work, however, as foxes often lie out during spells of fine warm weather. It is usual for main breeding earths to be stunk out before the beginning of the season, or stopped until it is time for them to be used again in the spring.

Cards are sent to earth-stoppers before a Meet, giving them their instructions, and although there is an element of routine about the whole thing, it is possible that a sudden change of wind may necessitate last minute alterations being made. A drastic change of wind may cause the Master to consider that foxes would in all probability run in exactly the opposite direction to that anticipated.

The whole question of earth-stopping can present a Master of Hounds with some of his biggest headaches. However much trouble he takes, there are bound to be places that are left open, and it stands to reason that new places will continually be discovered, especially after a dry summer.

Old prints tend to show the earth-stopper on his pony carrying a hurricane lantern at dead of night with spade over his shoulder, and one or two rough-looking terriers running by his side. In fact a small terrier is a very useful partner for the earth-stopper for, if for instance he wants to stop a drain, it is only humane to run a dog through it first, thus ensuring that it contains no inhabitant that would starve to death if the drain were closed, whether it be fox, rabbit or cat.

It is a good plan for the earth-stopper to visit the main earths again early in the morning, just to make sure that no one has tampered with his work of the night before. It is quite possible that water may have washed through or animals – perhaps a rabbit, another fox or even a badger – may have tried to scratch their way in and so the stones and faggots he used may either have been completely removed, or so much disturbed as to make an adequate entry for a hard-pressed fox later on in the day.

In the spring, of course, it is better not to stop out, otherwise the vixens will not be able to get in to feed their young. A vixen will leave her young after having suckled them, and sit nearby where she can keep watch without having to endure their constant scratching and worrying, in just the same way that a bitch will leave her whelps as they get older. If the earth is put to too late, the vixen will not be able to get in to feed her young. Of course, should for some reason a vixen with young be killed, then every endeavour must be made to find them, even though their chance of survival, even with the most willing foster-mother, is small. If, however, the cubs have reached the age of three to four months, it is quite possible that the dog-fox may bring them up.

Places where a keeper has known a vixen to lay cubs up, that are not really main earths, should be stunk out and stopped permanently for the winter and opened up again in the spring to prevent foxes from lying there. They can then be stopped during the early visits, and thus there will only be the big main earth to stop at night. Any place that a vixen has evidently scratched out with a view to laying up cubs should be left open after 1 February. Vixens will often litter down in snug gorse coverts, but there is always the risk of the cubs being killed by a stray dog, unless she has had the sense to utilise a handy rabbit hole.

Efficient earth-stoppers, like all other efficient helpers of the Hunt, must be valued and cherished for, as is so often the way with people versed in country lore, they tend to be a race of men born to the work. Nowadays much of the stopping is done by gamekeepers, and my own country is no exception.

Earths should be stopped with faggots tied round tightly with wire and a good stake through the middle with a hook at the end so they can be pulled out easily when unstopping. A pile of these faggots can be left in a handy place near an earth to save carrying them around. A faggot-stopped earth will generally keep a badger out, but the tendency is for stoppers to prefer the spade, as a fox can scratch out or in and reopen them, and then the stopper does not have to turn out to unstop in the evening after hunting. I must emphasize here that *unstopping* is just as important as efficient stopping.

In the old days many countries used to pay an earth-stopper a regular salary, and then fine him half-a-crown each time a fox went to ground in a *known* earth. My earth-stoppers have an annual feast at Badminton which is a very merry affair when I lead the singing, after which they are presented with a fee on the production of their pile of earth-stopping cards.

In countries where earths are scarce it is sometimes found necessary to make artificial earths, to provide somewhere for local foxes to have their cubs: in other words, for breeding purposes. Another advantage of artificial earths is that in grass countries where the coverts tend to be small and scattered it is useful to have snug earths judiciously placed at regular intervals, thus persuading foxes to take a good line. An additional advantage is that if an artificial earth is left open, it will only take a few minutes to bolt a fox. Also if it is a blank day, one knows where to go with some certainty of finding a fox.

However, before considering the possibility of making artificial earths, it must be pointed out that they must be put in places where they can be watched, as fox poaching is getting more and more prevalent, their pelts fetching exorbitant prices; and that the whole subject of artificial earths is extremely controversial. In this book I only wish to touch on the subject, and to tell you what my grandfather had to say.

He felt that artificial earths should be primarily intended as breeding establishments, and so among the chief points to be borne in mind should be the aspect, position, soil, drainage and materials used for their construction. When thinking of aspect, it was necessary to consider the habits of a young cub. He does not come out of the bowels of the earth until he is about four or five weeks old, and then generally only for an hour or two after sunrise in the morning, and then again for another hour just before sunset. The sun has great health-giving powers for young animals, therefore my grandfather said that the mouths of these man-made earths should be placed where they would catch as much sun as possible. At the same time, they would have not only to be sheltered from the prevailing winds, but more especially from those blowing from the north.

One of my earth-stoppers, Mr Fred Ind

Because for some weeks after emerging from the earth, the fox-cub youngsters keep close to its mouth, gambolling and playing within a radius of a very few yards, great care would have to be taken to see that the ground around the mouth of the earth was as dry as possible, for the little creatures would often play until they got hot and lay down exhausted. If the ground were at all swampy it was thought in my grandfather's day that the cubs would be liable to get what was then commonly known as the 'yellows' – a canine form of jaundice. This is not so prevalent nowadays but, even so, damp certainly does harm young creatures and if they do get cold they are certainly liable to pick up any infections that are hanging about.

My grandfather said that when choosing a position there were many things to take into account, thinking it a mistake for instance to put such an earth in the middle of gorse. For if it was made as it should be, well away from a ride or path, the earth-stopper would have great difficulty in locating it at dead of night when the gorse had grown up and he had no mark to guide him, with the result that he would be bound to wear a far too conspicuous regular path right across the earth. Added to this, foxes tend to lie above-ground in a gorse covert, so when the keeper went in to stop the earth at night he would disturb a fox for the following day's draw. He also thought that too little sun would reach it. To some extent, of course, those objections applied also to the making of artificial earths in any large coverts.

Next came the question of soil, a matter of careful selection, the main object being that the vixen should be provided with a dry place on which to lie and drop her cubs. It would also be an advantage if she could scratch or draw out a snug corner in the lodging-room to litter her offspring as her instinct, in common with that of many other animals, is to scratch out and make a bed for herself a few days before her confinement, preferring fresh soil for the purpose. By giving her the opportunity to follow her instincts, there would therefore be a far greater chance of her taking to her artificial home. My grandfather thought that chalk was by far the best soil for the purpose, as it is easily moved by a burrowing animal and therefore not so likely to cave in as gravel or sand.

Drainage was also important, but all my grandfather said on the subject was that the lodging-room should be considerably higher than the mouth of the hole, and that the ground outside should have channels dug in it so that any lying water could run away.

To my grandfather's mind, therefore, the best artificial earth would be one on the north side of a spinney containing a small hollow or valley with tree-clad sides, and it should be built half-way up the bank so that the sun would reach it during the late afternoon and evening.

The Huntsman of the Cheshire Hounds, Johnny O'Shea, having a word with 'Togo', the earth-stopper (D. W. Killington)

He thought that both materials and construction should be rough with the resulting earth looking as natural as possible, the outside cuts of trees, old bricks, flints, being utilised – anything in fact that would prevent the ground from falling in. He also stressed the need for really narrow entrances to prevent cur-dogs from getting in, and said that of course there should be more than one opening, so that the fox could slip away if an enemy came on the scene.

> Rouse thee! Earth stopper! rouse thee from
> thy slumber!
> Get thee thy worsted hose and winter coat on,
> While the good housewife, crawling from her
> blanket,
> Lights thee thy lantern.
>
> Clad for thy midnight silent occupation,
> Mount thy old doghorse, spade upon thy shoulder,
> Wire hair'd Vixen, wheresoe'er thou wendest
> Ready to follow
>
> Though the chill rain drops, driven by the
> north wind,
> Pelt thy old jacket, soaking through and
> through thee,
> Though thy worn hackney, blind and broken
> winded,
> Hobble on three legs;
>
> Finish thy night-work well, or woe betide thee,
> If on the morrow irritated Huntsman,
> Back'd by a hundred followers in scarlet,
> Find the earths open!

R. E. Egerton Warburton

(above right) Gimcrack '70, champion doghound Peterborough and Honiton 1972

(below right) Warden '68, winner of stallion hound class, Peterborough and Honiton 1972

(overleaf, left to right) Harry and Eddie Somerset with their father, David Somerset, and myself in front of the house (Anthony Del Balso)

Beaufort
1972

15
Terriers

Before going on to the subject of digging, I would like to talk about terriers, their choice and training.

The name that immediately springs to mind when terriers are mentioned is that of Parson John ('Jack') Russell, the westcountry sporting clergyman of the last century whose name is used so loosely nowadays to describe almost any sort of terrier. There is, in fact, no such thing as a 'Jack Russell Terrier': it is a type. Russell himself bred to all shapes and sizes according to his particular needs, and used any stock that met his own high standards, good working qualities being his main criterion.

The late Lord Poltimore, who was a great friend of mine, said that if Parson Russell saw a likely dog he would acquire him, having no special strain of his own. If he found his new acquisition suited to his work, he would breed from him. When the parson died, he left all his terriers to Nicholas Snow, Master of the Exmoor Foxhounds which were then – and still are – known as the Stars of the West. Nicholas Snow in turn left his kennel to Arthur Heinemann, who was in fact noted for never breeding from anything but his own strain, and was also a close friend of Lord Poltimore. It is therefore possible in occasional cases to trace a terrier's pedigree back to the sporting parson's breeding – indeed I have such a dog, Ajax, whose pedigree goes back to the 1860s, and whose grandfather was given to me by Miss Theodora Guest, another friend of Arthur Heinemann.

(above left) There is no need to extol the delights of hunting in Ireland! Here are the Kilkenny hounds in full cry (J. Meads)

(below left) The Meet at Brokenborough, February 1972. I think Peter Farquhar and David Harrison-Allen are talking behind me (Anthony Del Balso)

I have heard it said that Russell used a bull terrier for breeding purposes, but the following extract from *A Memoir of the Rev. John Russell of Tordown* written by his contemporary, E. W. L. Davies, should help to refute this assertion:

I seldom or ever see a real fox-terrier nowadays, said Russell recently to a friend who was inspecting a dog show containing a hundred and fifty entries under that denomination; they have so intermingled strange blood with the real article that, if he were not informed, it would puzzle Professor Bell himself to discover what race the so-called fox-terrier belongs to. And pray, how is it managed? inquired the friend, eager to profit by Russell's long experience in such matters.

The process, replied Russell, is simply as follows: they begin with a smooth bitch terrier; then, to obtain a finer skin, an Italian greyhound is selected for her mate. But as the ears of the produce are an eyesore to the connoisseur, a beagle is resorted to, and then little is seen of that unsightly defect in the next generation. Lastly, to complete the mixture, the bulldog is now called on to give the necessary courage; and the composite animals, thus elaborated, become, after due selection, the sires and dams of the modern fox-terriers.

The bulldog blood thus infused imparts courage, it is true, to the so-called terrier; he is matchless at killing any number of rats in a given time; will fight any dog of his weight in a Westminster pit; draw a badger heavier than himself out of his long box; and turn up a tom-cat possessed even of ten lives, before poor pussy can utter a wail. But the ferocity of that blood is in reality ill suited – nay, is fatal – to fox-hunting purposes; for a terrier that goes to ground and fastens on his fox, as one so bred will do, is far more likely to spoil sport than promote it; he goes in to kill, not to bolt, the object of his attack.

My own idea of a terrier is that his head should be of medium length, allowing plenty of room for brains. His jaw should be strong and square with good level teeth; and I prefer my terriers to have dark eyes with plenty of fire and intelligence in them; a broadish, deep chest with sloping shoulders and strong quarters. He should be well ribbed-up and should carry his stern up, but not so high that it bends over; nor should it be cut so short that there is not enough left to grab hold of. He should have strong, short straight legs in comparison with the size of his body, with plenty of bone; compact feet with a good hard pad, and shortish toes with very strong nails.

Terriers really enjoy their work. Mr Charles Parker of the Heythrop (John Tarlton)

When fit, he should not carry too much weight and, of course, he must be well muscled up. I do not think that a leggy dog is any good underground in my country for, although he may get into an earth or drain easily enough, once there he will be so cramped for space that he is not much use. I know there are plenty of people who would disagree with me, their argument being that dogs tuck their legs up.

His coat should be thick, hard and dense so that the water will run off him without penetrating, rather like a door-mat. Undoubtedly, in country where there is much plough and an abundance of wet drains, a smooth-coated dog is going to keep cleaner and will get dry much more quickly than his rough-coated fellow. He should be straight in the back, bright and lively.

One must not generalise too much, as it is impossible that any one type of terrier that is to work with foxhounds can be found equally good for every type of country. That is why Jack Russell bred them all shapes and sizes. Opinions vary, and everyone who has aspirations to being a terrier man naturally has his own particular favourite, depending on the sort of country in which the animal is going to be

expected to work. For instance with the Fell packs, when the terriers go with the Huntsman and Whipper-in on foot they need to be longer in the leg, not only for that reason, but because hill foxes tend to 'den' in rocky cairns. Thus when the terrier reaches his quarry, he often finds the fox perched on a ledge far above his head. In those circumstances, a short-legged terrier is going to find himself at a severe disadvantage, for in trying to scramble up to get to grips he is going to be badly punished as the fox holds the commanding position. It is also important that terriers used in that sort of country should be narrow in the shoulder, for they need to squeeze between rocky clefts. One with broad shoulders would be unable to get in, and therefore totally unsuitable for that kind of work.

Lord Poltimore, when he was Master of the Dulverton Foxhounds, used the small type of Devonshire working terrier and, in common with Russell, considered that the only pedigree of any value was a working one. He liked his terriers as light as possible, consistent with stamina, with good neck and shoulders; but he always used to say that a chesty type of terrier was useless in his Exmoor hill country, for much the same reasons as I have already described.

In defining exactly what a good working terrier should be, it is obvious that he must be one that will go to ground to fox or badger, and not merely be a dog that will kill rats or hunt out rabbits.

It is a fallacy to say that a terrier cannot be too hard, for what use is a dog that goes boldly into a great earth, gets up to his fox and then takes hold? He will become silent, unable to throw his tongue, so you have no idea where to dig and by the time you have eventually found him, he will probably either have killed the fox (and who wants to dig down to a dead fox at the end of a run?) or sustained bad injuries himself; and heaven help him if he meets a badger.

I think it is both fair and true to say that no one can really tell a game terrier just by looking at him, though a prominent dark eye is a good pointer. A trial to ground is the only acid test. It does not follow that just because a dog is bad-tempered and quarrelsome he will readily go to ground, and once there be of use. Very frequently such dogs do not prove to be game, and indeed are just as likely to be cowards.

Undoubtedly the terrier is an indispensable adjunct to the Hunt establishment, though I do not expect the galloping and jumping contingency to agree with me. I think it is true to say that ninety per cent of the people who hunt in the Shires for instance, are there

A nice collection of Border Terriers belonging to Mr Harold Watson of the Lunesdale Hunt (Frank H. Meads)

to gallop and jump, though undoubtedly they get a thrill from the sound of the horn and the cry of the hounds. It is the remaining ten per cent who are what I would class as hound men – and a real hound man is more likely to go to less fashionable packs for his sport. This leaves very few to enjoy the undoubted pleasures of terrier work.

If you want a terrier and your intention is to work him in the future, the best place to go for him is a Hunt kennel. Failing this, you should go to a known breeder of good working terriers, and preferably one who enters his terriers himself. It is not wise policy to buy a full-grown or entered animal, for you will nearly always find that there is something wrong with him – otherwise why would the owner be either willing or wishing to part with his animal?

The choice of a puppy is up to you, but I like to watch a litter playing and then pick one that seems to be full of character and confidence. There is an old-fashioned method which, in fact, applies to the choice of all puppies; and that is to remove the pups from their dam and see which one she fetches back first. Her favourite is likely to be the best of the litter from the point of view of general gameness and character, though not necessarily for looks.

I personally like my terriers to be with me as much as possible and see no reason why they should not be kept in the house as members of the family, though I agree with the school of thought that asserts, that because the terrier is the perfect companion in both house and in the field, and full of charm and versatility, people have done their best to spoil it for work. When he degenerates into a mere household pet, it is easy to lose sight of the fact that he is basically a working dog.

It is necessary to train a working terrier as carefully as any other dog, in order to develop his natural ability for his work. Exactly the same fundamental rules apply to the training of terriers as to any other young animal, and should be based on a foundation of quiet kindly firmness. If you do find it necessary to punish your pupil, then do it properly: administer the beating with a cane and make him yelp. You will find that you have taught him a salutary lesson that he will probably remember all his life. Ever after, a certain scolding note in your voice will be enough – but you must never overlook any act of disobedience.

It is the greatest mistake to enter your terrier to rabbits. There are some terriers that are intelligent enough to know when they are being entered to fox and will then ignore rabbits, but it is a great bore to have to spend an hour or two moving a ton or so of earth

Good hunt terriers come in all shapes and sizes! (D. Doble)

Gone to ground! Hunting with the East Devon (Sport & General)

when digging up your terrier, and then find it lying up to a rabbit.

A dog should never be permitted to chase cats, for sooner or later he will kill one, and then the trouble will begin. Ten to one it will be the pride and joy of one of your closest neighbours – and erstwhile friends – and a feud will have been started that, like Tennyson's brook, could go on for ever.

The best age to enter your terrier to fox is when it is just over a year old, which means that if you have a summer puppy you can take it cub-hunting the following year. Each Hunt has its own regular terrier man, and as you can only in any case be out by courtesy of the Master, it is important that you should wait in the wings so to speak. First of all make friends with the terrier man, and then you must hope that you will be invited to enter your puppy. In the meantime, let him watch experienced terriers at several digs before he has a go himself. When the time comes, wait until they have dug right down to the fox, then pull out the Hunt terrier and quickly substitute your own puppy. Be quiet and non-committal about the whole business – in other words, neither encourage nor force him. You will find that it is all in the breeding and, if that is right, in he will go, and a moment later your ears will be rejoiced by the sound of him baying.

If he dashes in too quickly, you must get him out as fast as you can, because it is not worth risking his being punished at this early stage. If all goes well, let him lie baying for a minute or two before you haul him out and make a great fuss of him. When the fox is dead and out, he can be allowed to join in the worry and fight for his share of the quarry. A word of warning here – you must be very careful at first if he is a coloured terrier for until hounds have got used to him, they could easily mistake him for a fox in the general mêlée. You must not run the slightest risk of a sudden pounce and a scrunch, for that would spell the end of your terrier.

If he proves slow to enter do not worry overmuch, for this is where patience brings its own reward. A dog that takes his time very often proves to be one of the best in the end.

Another word of warning is never to forget the cardinal rule that only one terrier should go to ground at a time. If two meet face to face, they may mistake one another for a fox and fight to the death. Also a second terrier will very likely get behind the first, and push the unfortunate creature on to the fox, and it will be savagely punished.

16
Digging

To dig or not to dig, that is the question! And a very burning one it is. At all times it is a decision that has to be made by the Master, and by him alone. During the cub-hunting time he can please himself, but as soon as the hunting season proper starts he will find that his decisions have to be governed by quite different factors from those he had to consider during the autumn months, and he may well find himself being criticised, and reasonably so, if he insists on too many digs, and ones that go on too long.

During the cub-hunting season digging out a cub is a matter of policy in the education of the young entry, and the cub should by and large always be dug out and eaten by the hounds unless very good reasons can be put forward for not so doing. If a cub is marked to ground early in the morning in an impossible place that will take two hours and preferably a bulldozer or a gang of Irish navvies to break into, then it is obvious that it would be better for hounds to go on and find another cub than to hang around waiting indefinitely. But that earth must, of course, be stopped before hounds draw again.

If the Master decides to leave a digging party behind to deal with the cub, firstly it is most important that he puts somebody who knows what he is about in charge of the operation. I will be talking about that later. Secondly, he must give direct orders as to what is ultimately to be done with the cub – whether he is to be shot, or allowed to escape if there is no chance of hounds returning to eat him.

If, on the other hand, hounds mark a cub to ground after a good morning's work, then the Master must be prepared for a good long dig, at the end of which not only will he be able to blood his hounds, but they will also have learned a lesson on how to mark their foxes to ground.

After 1 November the question of whether to dig or not becomes far more complicated, and the Master has to make his decision in the light of several factors. First he must take into consideration the scenting conditions, then the weather and the time of day and, lastly, he has to make a rough estimate as to how long the job is likely to take.

On a good scenting day before Christmas when the hours of daylight are all too short, unless he is certain that the dig will take only a few minutes and that there is a good prospect of bolting the fox, he would be wise to go on and find another one. If he therefore decides not to dig, he must have the hounds called away as quickly as possible, and leave the earth quietly, disclosing its presence to as few people as possible. It is not a good plan to provide a crowd of amateurs with an afternoon's earth digging, when in all probability they will not know what they should do when they ultimately reach their target.

If the scent is so poor that there is little prospect of another good run, the weather is clement, and there is likely to be sufficient daylight, then I think I would go ahead and dig, even during the regular season. This is one of the many subjects though on which there can be no hard and fast rules, and every Master must use his own discretion, making up his mind for himself, and then abiding by his decision.

Digging out a fox is not just a matter of brute strength and the ability to ply a spade, pickaxe or shovel. It is an art in itself and, like all skills, has to be learnt.

If you are going to do terrier work before you start out in the morning, it is as well to make sure that you have the necessary tools to hand. You will need a good sharp graft, a shovel, a mattock, a long-handled billhook and a set of drain-rods, two or three sacks (difficult to come by nowadays with plastic so predominant), a piece of board, some binder twine and always a sharp knife. Check each time you go out that your tools are in good order, and that you have a rubber torch with a spare battery, and a dry place for it. It is essential that you should wear a stout pair of leather boots.

In all probability most of the people concerned will know – or certainly think they know – quite a bit about digging, but if they allow themselves to get involved in too heated a discussion as to the ways and means, very likely crafty old Reynard is making good his escape! At every dig there must be one person and one alone who is in charge of operations, and preferably he should be someone whom the Master has deputed for the task. When it is settled who that person is going to be, everybody else must agree to obey him and do exactly what he wishes.

The first thing to remember when digging for a fox is to stop all the other holes. Ram branches down them and pack earth in between or on top. If you just fill up the holes with earth, you will be asking for the mortifying sight of your fox running fast away from you down the hillside when you have perhaps been digging for a couple of hours, for a fox can easily scratch his way through earth. It is therefore well worth taking the greatest care to check that every possible exit is blocked efficiently.

Before you put in a terrier, insert a long flexible stick up the pipe so that you can see which way it runs, leaving this stick in. Then if the soil crumbles, the pipe can still be found. Whatever happens, before you enter a terrier you must also remember to take off his collar, as it is all too easy for it to get caught up in a root or stone, and then the poor little brute can choke to death several feet underground without anyone being any the wiser.

As I said before, but it is worth repeating, never make the mistake of letting two terriers get into an earth at once, as not only will you have the greatest difficulty in keeping a check on where they are, but they may find themselves face to face, mistake each other for the fox, and go straight into the attack with dire consequences.

When you hear your dog baying, do not start to dig immediately, as this may only make him move further underground, taking the fox with him. When the baying has come consistently from the same place for several minutes, then is the time for action.

It is most important that you should leave enough space to work, so make it a golden rule to start really wide from the outset. A hole begins on the surface, and even though at first a foot-wide trench may seem to be sufficient, you will find that as soon as the pipe starts getting deeper, even two feet is not nearly enough to ensure that there is sufficient room for the diggers to wield their spades. Keepers are the worst offenders in this respect, as they are so used to the restrictions of ferreting that they tend to begin with a tiny trench on the surface and are therefore obliged to start all over again, widening the trench that they have already cut.

Start with two diggers, one who stands over the pipe opening it up, and the other who shovels the earth clear, thus keeping the hole open. It is very important to keep the hole open so that you ensure that the terrier gets enough air, and this must be done by digging below the level of the pipe. The man who is cutting out the top layer should wait until the man with the shovel has cleared it again, in case by working too fast and out of unison he should inadvertently block the hole.

It is very important not to 'crown in'. This may be found successful when ferreting rabbits, but is not a method to use when digging a fox. Take just that little bit longer and follow the pipe, for you should not rely on seeing which way the hole runs and then expect to crown down, for you could all too easily come down into another pipe, or else find that the terrier has gone into a branch line that breaks off before your 'crowning-in' hole. There is nothing for it then but to start all over again, which is a great waste of time and effort. While you must dig as quickly as possible, you must not forget to stop at frequent intervals to listen for the terrier, as it is quite possible that he may be tucked away in a side pipe, and you could have over-shot him and possibly already even have filled it in.

Naturally, when hounds are there, as soon as you get to him, the fox will be despatched with a humane killer, and the carcass then drawn out and thrown to the hounds. If you are on your own with-out hounds, then again you must shoot the fox the moment you get down to him. If a humane killer is not available, you will have to despatch him with a sharp blow on the head, bearing in mind before ever you start digging the need to have a suitable object for the purpose that will come quickly to hand.

Getting a fox out of a drain presents far fewer problems because you will know exactly where he is. Put your terrier in, remembering, as I said before, first to take off his collar and then, when you can hear him, open the drain just behind where he is baying. He will probably move on, and you will then need to open the drain again and so on, repeating the process until the fox eventually reaches the stopped end of the drain and is forced to come to a halt.

It is sometimes possible to get hold of a fox in a drain without resorting to the spade. Go quietly to one end and block the opening with your feet – never forget to wear those stout leather boots – or with a piece of board (which I mentioned at the outset as one of the prerequisites for the task in hand). Keep as quiet as you can, and give the signal for the terrier to be released down the drain. Then, with a bit of luck, the fox will back towards you until you can get hold of him by the brush. You must seize the brush with your left hand, getting hold of the two hindlegs in your right hand. Then you must pull him back very gently, making absolutely sure that you keep your foot (in its suitable leather boot!) against his body so that he is pushed tight against the side of the hole. As he gradually comes out, you must let go of his brush and slide your left hand up his back until you reach his shoulder blades. Then with a swift movement, you must reach up and grab him by the scruff of the neck as high up as you possibly can, in the same way that you would catch a rat or a cat. Reverse hands from the outset if you think you will manage the operation better that way. Should he come down mask first, he is certain to turn the moment he sees you, and then you must race into action, grabbing him firmly by the brush.

If you find it impossible to get your fox to bolt from the drain, you will need your drain-rods. When you have fitted them together, tie a sack that you have padded well with hay or grass over the end so that it will act like a ramrod, making sure that your padded sack is both full and wide enough to fill the hole completely, otherwise the fox will ride on it. Push this improvised ramrod slowly and gently forward a yard at a time with a thrusting movement. This will mean that although the fox will not be hurt, he will inevitably come out like a cork from a bottle.

Never forget that your fox may well not be alone – in fact there could be as many as three or four foxes in that single drain. So when number one has gone away, keep your stoutly clad foot against the end until you have made absolutely certain that the drain is empty.

If your terrier has bolted one fox and is eager to get back in again, do not forget what I said in another part of this book: it is more than possible that the hunted fox is still in the drain and that the one that bolted was a fresh one. Your terrier's nose is not likely to deceive him – or you for that matter!

When you are putting together your equipment, do not forget to include some disinfectant in case of accidents, and you will find it easier if you dilute it before you start out. I prefer Dettol as it does not sting in the same way as iodine, and it will do for you as well as for your terrier. (Pettifer's green oils are a useful standby for the treatment of simple bites and cuts, these being oils to which a proportion of antiseptic has been added. Not only are they very soothing, but they cause superficial wounds to heal quickly and cleanly.) Do not forget that holes made by teeth heal from the inside, so they should be left open to drain if necessary. If your dog has any worse injury than the odd toothmark, you must take him straight away to a veterinary surgeon. And I repeat that you must always make sure that your dog's anti-tetanus injections are kept up-to-date.

Make a habit of keeping a big plastic carrier of fresh water and a deepish bowl in whatever vehicle you are using, so that your dog can have a good drink when he has been to ground, for you may have to move off too quickly to have time to find a nearby stream. When you get home, clean the mud off him and look him over, especially examining his eyes. These should be washed out either with a good eye lotion, warm weak tea (without milk!) or a saline solution which can be kept made up using one teaspoonful of salt to a pint of boiling water. It goes without saying that you must look after the comfort of your dog before you seek your own.

17

Horses and Stables in General

My grandfather said that the horse owner who knows nothing about horses is bound to be putting himself in a false position, especially when he has to depend upon a servant who may know little more, or who has prejudices and absurd traditions that can do as much mischief as sheer ignorance. Those words are just as true today as when they were written nearly a hundred years ago, and they will hold good as long as people employ others to care for their horses.

To own horses it is not necessary to have an elaborate knowledge of stables and stablecraft, but it is only prudent to make sure that you are reasonably well versed in the basic elements. When you find yourself at a loss, it is as well to know where you can go for sound advice. Someone among your friends is bound to be knowledgeable on the particular aspect where you find yourself lacking but, as I said when talking about hound breeding, I think here too it is a mistake to consult too many so-called 'experts', for conflicting advice only muddles, and is therefore of little use.

When you are engaging stable staff what you need are people who are capable of keeping your horses fit for the particular work they will be required to do in the light of your own circumstances – no more and no less. It is no good having a horse fed and exercised fit to win a steeplechase, if all you want to do is one day's hunting each week. Nor, however, on your one day do you want your horse to come to a shuddering halt due to lack of condition. I am, of course, now addressing myself to the novice owner who is aware of the yawning gaps in his knowledge of horses generally, and is sensible enough to recognise the fact.

There have been some excellent books written in the last ten years or so, for with modern materials even stablecraft has changed during that time, while the difference in feeding has been revolutionary. It would be as well to embark upon your career as a horse owner versed in modern technology. For myself, I feel that the old and trusted methods still have much to commend them.

I am very fortunate in that my range of stables at Badminton are ideal for their purpose: there is plenty of room, and all the work can be carried out under cover, which is saving in manpower and improves efficiency. They have been self-contained since the complex was altered and modernised in 1878 with money raised from the sale of my father's commission in the Blues.

No loose box is smaller than ten by twelve feet, and they are all fifteen feet high, with good windows and ventilation – I consider that fresh air is vital for a horse's well-being. It is true that some grooms like to have warm stables, for horses living in such an atmosphere tend to have beautifully smooth and glossy coats and layers of fat which, to the uneducated eye, appear to be rippling muscle. Such a man would very likely water his charges only at stated times, as he would feel that by so doing they would tend to drink less, their beds would keep drier, and therefore he would not need to do so much mucking out. He would be wrong, for it has been found in tests that a horse will drink about eight gallons daily if watered twice a day, but only about five gallons if water is always available. In my stables there are automatic water troughs which can, of course, be turned off when necessary to stop horses from drinking too much when they are over-heated. These are a fairly recent innovation, and save a great deal of time and labour.

The floors of my stables are laid perfectly flat, and there are no drains of any sort. This arrangement has stood the test of time and I think it is ideal by any standards. A horse that has to stand on a slope all the time must eventually show signs of strain, and channels and drains can lead to all sorts of additional troubles.

There is a wall-mounted manger for the feed in the corner of each box, and my Stud-groom, Brian Higham, who thinks that fibre is essential for a horse's well-being, never stints good hay as he says that a prime cause of colic is the feeding of oats or young grass without a good amount of hay to help it safely through the system. He prefers to have it put on the ground as this not only obviates the need for filling nets, a tedious and time-consuming business, but also enables the horses to feed with their heads at a natural level. They are not giraffes, and it is better therefore for them not to have to reach up to a rack, when dust and hayseeds are bound to get in their eyes and ears. People criticise this practice of putting hay on the

A horse's health begins with his feet (John Tarlton)

ground as being wasteful, but a horse is just as likely to leave hay in his net, and we find that very little is trampled into the bedding. If a hay-net is used, then it is very important to make absolutely certain that it is tied really securely, though with a quick-release knot, well above the ground, so that your treasured animal cannot possibly catch a foot in it and so get cast.

Hay should be a good colour – nearly the same as it was when it was first baled. This colour should be general throughout the load. It should be composed of a good mixture of grasses, and be free of

Removing a worn shoe (John Tarlton)

thistles and other coarser growths. If possible, there should be a sprinkling of flowers in it, and they should have remained much the same colour as they were when they were growing, especially the yellow ones. The hay should be sweet and fragrant to the nose, and completely free from any sour or bitter smell. It should be soft and silky in texture, and fairly long, and it should never be brittle or dusty. Should you be obliged to have coarser hay, then you would be wise to keep it for a time if possible, as it will improve with age.

In the old days, we employed a man as a feeder, that being his sole responsibility, but times have changed, and now my Stud-groom is entirely responsible for feeding all my horses. In many ways I think the present system is better, as the Stud-groom goes out with the horses himself, and is therefore in a position to assess more accurately exactly how each individual horse needs to be fed. Brian Higham likes to feed three or, better still, four times a day, but keeps down the amount of oats or nuts, as he thinks that a hunter in work needs a surprisingly small amount of concentrates. He sees that a bucket of linseed gruel is given to every horse after hunting. Horses love linseed and it is very beneficial, provided that the feeder understands its uses, for if it is allowed to stand too long it can become poisonous. It oils the works, so to speak, and gives horses good coats.

Brian Higham thinks – and I agree with him wholeheartedly – that there are no short cuts to good horse management and that every horse is an individual and should be treated as such. A horse, like most other animals, expects and thrives on a strict routine. He requires a specific amount of time spent on him; so to develop good methods which need not necessarily take longer than slipshod ways, is mainly a question of self-discipline rather than of the hours available. Those who are not prepared or able to devote enough time to his care should leave horse-keeping to others.

There is no doubt that wheat straw is far and away the best bedding, but regular skipping is equally essential for a good bed. Many people use various systems of deep-litter nowadays, but I

Blacksmiths travel long distances with mobile forges to ensure that horses get hot shoes (Frank H. Meads)

know very little about this subject. When it is cleared out, as it has to be from time to time, it makes a very heavy load, and I am told that it tends to be damp, and may not therefore be very good for the horses' feet.

My Hunt horses are got up in July and ridden individually at road work for six weeks. Once they are hunting and fit, riding out is done in pairs with one horse on a leading rein. Horses that miss their turn hunting are worked individually.

On hunting days, we nearly always take out second horses, as a horse can do many more short days and remain fit than one called upon to do long, gruelling days when it is perhaps out of the stables for nine or ten hours. I repeat that all horse masters agree it is the time that a horse is *out of its own stable* that tells on him in the long run. My horses are called upon to do two half-days a week, though the Huntsman's horses naturally have a harder time, being ridden both harder and further than the others.

My Stud-groom's job, in common with all other Stud-grooms in a hunting stable, is to supply fit horses on hunting days for me and the members of my family, and for the hunt staff. One of Brian Higham's firm maxims is that long days kill horses, and this is a maxim that certainly seems to have led to longevity in my stables. The general reckoning in a hunting yard is that a horse should not be called on to do more than three full days a fortnight, but I know there are exceptions to this rule, as to every other, and some horses certainly need to have more work than others to be kept in proper shape.

Shoeing
At Badminton we employ our own farrier, but I would like to stress that it is worth travelling quite a long way in order to be absolutely sure that your horse is shod properly. It is truly the falsest economy to go to the man down the road just because he is handy, unless you are absolutely certain that he is a master at his craft – and craft it certainly is.

The well-being of a horse begins with his feet, and so the health of his hooves and the suitability of the shoes put on are most vital points, and are bound to make all the difference to the enjoyment of your hunting. Nothing can be more maddening than to lose a good hunt because of a loose or lost shoe, and when a good part of the foot comes away as well and the horse goes lame for several weeks, or even for the rest of the season, that is a disaster that must be avoided at all costs.

It is important to have some idea of shoeing yourself, and no

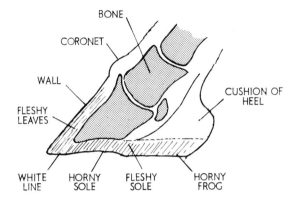

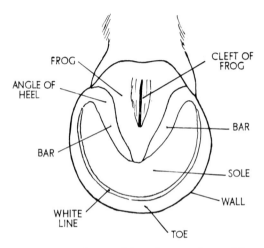

doubt there are several good books on the subject which you can read. Nobody, unless it is his job, can expect to be an expert on every aspect of horse management, but this is a case where a little knowledge is better than none at all. The following notes may be of use to you, together with diagrams of a horse's hoof: the upper figure is a section taken through the centre of the foot as it is seen when resting upon the ground; the lower one is the foot as viewed from beneath – in other words, the worm's eye view!

The horn or insensitive part of the wall of the foot is thickest at the toe and the heels, and thinner over the sides of the foot. It is much harder on the outside than it is as it merges with the horny leaves which dovetail into the fleshy leaves which form the sensitive part, these in turn being attached to the bones of the foot.

The sole is horny, but it becomes more and more sensitive the further from the ground it gets, and the fleshy inner sole supports

169

the horny sole, which it feeds. In turn, the horny sole protects the fleshy sole, and helps the walls of the foot to carry the weight of the horse. It is therefore important that it should not be pared, as it needs to be as strong and as thick as possible. What I will call the 'white line' is the point between the wall and the sole, where the fleshy and horny leaves connect, and no nail must go in beyond this line.

The frog is in the main a thick piece of horn growing from the fleshy frog above. One of its functions is to prevent the horse from slipping, another is to help bear the horse's weight and, by its india-rubber-like resilience, to act as a sort of shock-absorber, stopping the horse's legs and shoulders from being jarred to pieces every time he sets foot to the ground.

The horn of the hoof grows rapidly, but it also wears away very quickly when it comes into contact with hard ground, and that is why the horse needs to be shod regularly and well. A hunter will need shoeing when either his shoes have worn thin – and I cannot stress

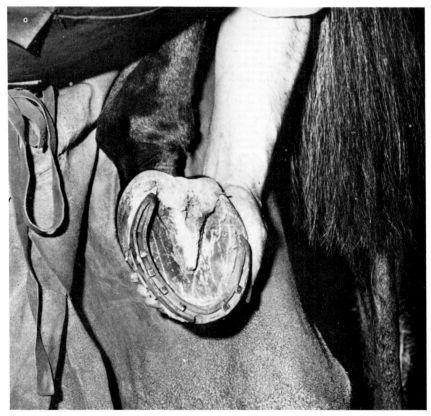

This shoe has been made short to prevent the horse from rubbing the other leg when exercising (John Tarlton)

enough the importance of personal attention to this unless like me, you have the good fortune to have a totally reliable Stud-groom – or when the horn has grown so much, perhaps because the horse has been doing very little work and has not worn the shoes down, that it is necessary to do what a farrier calls a remove. For this the shoes are taken off, the horn rasped down, and the same ones replaced. Generally speaking, with a normal amount of road work, you should expect shoes to last three or four weeks.

The actual process of shoeing deserves a mention, for if you know something about this, you will be in a better position to judge whether the job is being done expertly. First the old shoe is taken off, while a new shoe is made that will exactly fit the individual horse's foot – ready-made shoes are never the same – and then the new growth of horn should be rasped down and the bearing surface of the wall levelled. Any flakes of horny shoe that would eventually come away of their own accord should be removed. The hot, made shoe is then placed on the foot for a moment or two and, when it is taken away, it will have burnt the wall brown where it has touched. These burnt places show the farrier where he must rasp down until a complete all-round contact is achieved. Then the hot shoe is put on the foot again, and this time it is nailed to the foot, the nails being clinched, or knocked sideways, where they stick out through the wall. These points are, in fact, known as 'clinches', and they have to be rasped down until they are completely smooth. The rasp should then be run round between the junction of the hoof and the shoe, this being called finishing. This bevels the hoof and prevents any possibility of its splitting.

It is a good idea to watch the farrier at work, and you must keep an eagle eye open to see that he does not either pare the horny sole or slice the frog, for both of these practices are absolutely wrong. You must also see that the rasping is done to the weight-bearing part of the foot and not to the toe, as is sometimes done in order to make the foot fit the shoe, rather than the other way round. This practice narrows the horn wall, and thus makes it almost impossible to find a holding place for a nail. You should also watch to see that the hot shoe is not held on the foot for more than a second or two. If it is, you will know that that is the lazy way, for it is done with the intention of burning away the projections which should, of course, be properly rasped. The burnt portions soon crumble away, and the end result is a badly fitting shoe.

Shoes that are too wide for the foot are liable to catch the opposite leg, while fore-shoes that are too long at the heel can be struck off by the toe of the hind-shoe. Shoes that are too short at the heel can lead to bruising.

The number of nails driven in depends necessarily to a great extent upon the nature of the country. In very deep countries it is essential to have four nails on the outside and three on the inside, whereas in light, chalky places, five altogether may be found to be enough. If you are going to take your horse for a few days' hunting elsewhere, it would be as well to check on this point – lost shoes ruin hunting holidays.

If your farrier pricks, ie drives the point of the nail too deep and thus pricks the sensitive leaves, or if he presses, again driving the nail too deep but not quite deep enough to prick the leaves, merely pressing upon them – he should not be given a second chance.

There are various types of shoe. First there is the 'fullered', which is one with a groove, or possibly two, in the ground surface of the shoe. This not only gives a better foothold, but is also lighter. You will find however that it will wear out more quickly, as the nail can only be supported on two sides instead of all round as in the case of a stamped hole in a plain shoe.

A concave shoe, which can also be fullered, is a common hunter shoe. Here the ground surface is narrower than the bearing surface making the shoe lighter, but again it cannot last as long as a plain shoe.

A seated shoe is the opposite to a concave shoe, and is used on horses with very flat soles, as it prevents the shoe from bearing on the sole. This is not suitable for deep-going, and should only be used where strictly necessary.

For horses that brush, a feather-edged shoe should be used, and a shoe with a bar across the back and slightly raised heels is intended to take the pressure off tendons and protect against cracks that can appear as a result of an injury known as quarter cracks.

All in all, no horse should be expected to carry more than twelve ounces of shoe on each foot.

Saddlery and Bitting

I would like to say about saddlery generally that it is not worth investing in stuff of inferior quality. Not only will it have to be replaced more often, but its safety qualities will not be of the highest standard. So always choose stainless steel rather than nickel, and of course good quality leather; never buy anything plastic, except perhaps buckets for use in the stable.

Meticulous care has to be taken in the cleaning of saddlery, using a good saddle soap to maintain the suppleness of all the leather. As saddlery has perforce to stand up to all weathers, and is liable to spend half its time wet through, it is essential that a place must be provided where it can be dried slowly and steadily so that the leather will not harden and crack or split. In my own saddle room we have an ingenious fixture which is, in effect, a long radiator pipe with a wooden saddle-horse built along its complete length. The saddles can therefore be placed on a warm surface, enabling them to be gradually dried right through.

All saddlery must be inspected regularly, and any worn parts immediately be repaired if possible, or replaced. This is a chore that must not be neglected, for a broken strap, rein or stirrup-leather could have fatal consequences.

Wet rugs hanging around are the bane of many households, so a covered shed with a through-draught where lines can be put up is an invaluable adjunct to any Hunt stable. Rugs also have to be washed from time to time, so provision must be made for this operation.

When buying a saddle, it is essential to see that it fits the horse, and that the horse is not expected to fit the saddle. You should either take the horse to the saddler or ask the saddler to visit you, so that you can ensure that a proper fit is effected. A good saddler will be able to make any necessary alterations.

Where bitting is concerned, it has always been said that there is an answer to every horse's mouth, but I do not feel it is my place to give much advice on this highly complex and controversial subject. Suffice to say that even the most diabolically violent bit has very little real mechanical stopping power. Bits act in the main by an association of ideas, certain bits being used for specific purposes: possibly to get a horse's head higher or lower, perhaps to restrain a tendency for the horse to be over-bent or to stretch his neck out too far and for a multitude of other reasons. It may be that you will prefer to experiment by trial and error, but again there are plenty of good books on the subject, and many people to consult who fancy themselves as experts. What I do think, though, is that a snaffle-mouthed horse is a figment of someone's imagination, as the expression should denote a horse that will bend at the poll and flex the lower jaw at the behest of a snaffle only, and this is an impossibility. You may find that you have a horse that *goes* well in a snaffle, but that is a matter of personal taste and opinion. For my own part, I like a double bridle, but I am quite prepared to admit that this is because it is what I have always been accustomed to.

Some notes about the use of the curb written by David Brock,

MFH, have always seemed to me to contain excellent advice, as well as making good sense:

> The action of the curb is that of a lever with a movable fulcrum, or point of pivot; the fulcrum varies according to the force employed. When the curb is at rest, the fulcrum is the point of contact between the bit and the bars of the mouth. When tension is applied by the reins, the bottom of each cheek moves backwards, and the top moves forward until it is stopped either by the bit-stall reaching the forward limit of its travel, or else by the tightening of the curb-chain. In the former case the bit will now pivot about its point of attachment to the bit-stall – that is, the topmost point of the cheek – and the bit will slide up into the corners of the mouth; probably it will lift the curb-chain as it goes up, and will cause pain by bringing the chain into contact with the very sensitive area above the chain groove. But if the curb-chain comes into play before the bit-stall, it, by becoming taut, arrests the forward movement of the upper end of the cheek. As the reins apply further tension, the bit will pivot about the point where the curb-chain is attached to the bit, and the latter will move backward against the bars of the mouth, causing, in the properly mouthed horse, the desired flexion. If the curb-chain is in the correct position, it will remain in the chin-groove and cause no discomfort. But should it slide up even the minutest amount it will cause discomfort or pain, and acting as it does beneath the jaw with an upward effect, will negative the action of the bit on the bars – which is a downward action, causing the flexion. So, in fitting the curb-bit the chain must fit exactly in the groove, and it must be tight enough to act before the forward movement of the upper cheek is stopped by the bit-stall. Just about three links tighter than you think is too tight; a slack curb-chain being neither efficient nor humane. The chin-groove in which the chain should rest, is lined with comparatively insensible gristle. There should therefore be no risk of its being rubbed sore, and, in fact, it practically never is; the wash-leather and leather guards which are sometimes put at the back of the chain (*many people nowadays use a piece of sheep-skin*) can only be of use if the chain is incorrectly fitted and rides up over the groove on to the sensitive surface above. A lip-strap is advisable, for it prevents the chain from riding up, and also obviates any risk of a jerk of the horse's head reversing the bit in his mouth. It passes through the ring attached to the centre of the chain.

I would like to say a word or two about a Pelham, which is simply a snaffle and curb less one mouth-piece; or perhaps I can describe it as David Brock does as 'a curb with a couple of snaffle-rings soldered on'. The action of the top rein raises the bit into the corner of the mouth, thus raising the head carriage. When this has happened, pressure should be relaxed on this rein so that the bit is allowed to drop in the mouth again until it is level with the bars, and then the other rein, in effect the curb-rein, can be brought into play.

David Brock also agrees with me and with my Stud-groom that the running martingale should be attached to the curb-reins as they tend to lower the head, while the snaffle-reins are meant to raise it; so it seems silly to put a lowering martingale on a rein that is designed to raise the head.

Clipping
In early times, horses were not clipped at all; then came the practice of shaving them with a long razor at the beginning of the season, which gave rise to a good deal of satire and ribald comment. Next horses were clipped with scissors and comb late in the season, and there were special men employed by Hunts for the purpose. After that came the hand-clipper, and then the wheel and mechanically propelled knife which had to be turned laboriously by hand. It is only in recent times that we have had the electric clipper which shortens the process and enables a far more efficient job to be done.

All my hunters in work are clipped every fourteen to twenty days, starting at the beginning of the season as soon as my Stud-groom thinks it necessary. He clips two or three horses each and every day himself, assisted by my Second Horseman. Brian Higham is convinced that frequent clipping makes for fitter horses, and it certainly eases grooming. After the first week in January, he uses the singeing lamp, and continues with it until the end of the season, clipping stopping after February.

He never resorts to dope in order to clip a horse, but this is where experience and good management come into the picture. He often cures a difficult horse very quickly by dint of stabling him next to the clipping box: another method he uses is to run the clippers over him regularly without actually cutting. He avoids the use of the twitch when possible, but says it is sometimes necessary. A twitch tends to make the horse break out, and the clipping has to stop until he has cooled down.

To mark out a horse for clipping, the first question is whether to leave the legs on, and whether a saddle-mark is necessary. Opinions differ, and there is a school of thought that considers the legs should be clipped out so that it is easier to see where thorns have penetrated. Another school of thought thinks that the longer coat acts as a protection. There is a similar difference of opinion about the saddle-mark, some considering it a protection, others thinking that it acts as a sort of poultice and takes a long time to dry. It is also thought to be a device that hides, or perhaps draws the eye away from, a long back. One system is to make a clean sweep of everything at the first two clippings, beginning towards the end of September – legs, saddle-mark and all. After that, the long blades can be used on the legs and saddle-mark, so that they are only lightly clipped.

For the hindlegs you start by measuring the full span of your hand, the tip of the thumb to the tip of the little finger, from the tip of the hock straight up the back of the leg. Then put your finger on the tip of the hock and stretch your hand up the back of the leg, and where your thumb touches you can start to clip. Run a straight line up the side of the leg so that it comes out just above the dimple of the stifle joint. For the foreleg you take a span from the bone that sticks out behind the knee and run a straight line up to the top of the forearm just where the hair curls into the chest.

You must always see that the knife travels against the hair and that it is all done very quietly. If necessary you can resort to a blindfold, and another method is to get your assistant to hold up one of the horse's forelegs (though I have known plenty of horses that can stand on two diagonal legs). A thing called a dealer's twitch is sometimes useful, this being a broad piece of string or stout tape which is put through the mouth and fastened tightly on the top of his head.

If a saddle-mark is to be left on, put the horse's saddle in its natural position and clip round it, finishing off the job by cleaning up the edges with a sharp pair of scissors. Round the tail you should make two clean lines, quite straight, which meet in the middle of his backbone and make him look smart.

After these first two clippings, you may prefer to run over the legs with the long blades, or with a pair of scissors and a comb – the old-fashioned method. The heels should never be clipped if the legs are left on; and the protective hair round the coronet and in the heels should always be left to prevent cracked heels.

A hogged mane should be taken off every couple of weeks. We always plait manes for hunting, the plaits being taken out when the horses come home. Excessive pulling of the tail is not necessary as, provided it is ended off neatly at the bottom and the long hairs are

Enjoying a well-earned rest at the end of the hunting season (H. R. Savage)

removed from the top, the horse will look quite as smart as the horse with an over-shaped tail, which tends to look rather unnatural and a little vulgar. When you are pulling a tail, start at the top and do not do too much at any one time or the tail may become sore. Besides you will probably take too much out, and the hair can only grow back, which is a lengthy process.

When you are clipping and trimming you must not take off eyelashes, whiskers or the hair inside the ears.

The horse's legs, feet, and hooves should not be washed as the water tends to run down the leg into the thousands of little ducts that run from the hoof-wall to the nerve centre in the frog, and if they get choked lameness can result. Over-oiling can produce the same effect.

Buying a Horse

This is an all-important business. To buy a horse is the easiest thing in the world, but to buy a good one is quite a different matter, and the old saying that a fool and his money are easily parted is appropriate in this context.

What you must always remember when making your choice is that not only must you choose a horse that is going to be suitable for

These brood mares are the sort of stock from which our future hunters will come
(Colin Simister)

the country where you are going to hunt, but he must be one that is suitable for you, on which you are going to feel happy and will therefore enjoy riding. Here again there are a few golden rules:

1   Never buy a horse without having him vetted.
2   Never buy one without a full and adequate trial, unless you feel that having watched his performance perhaps during the course of a season, you have been able to make a reasonable assessment of his suitability.
3   Never buy a horse in poor condition, for whereas he may be a nice quiet ride when he is poor, he is likely to be a totally different animal when full of the right kind of food and therefore feeling on top of the world.
4   Do not buy a horse just because you know he has carried a hunt servant well, particularly a Huntsman. The job he is now going to be asked to do will be totally different, and a horse that has become accustomed always to going out in front can be a well-nigh impossible ride when he has to be hitched up behind.
5   Always look at a horse's eye. A small and ungenerous one tends to denote cunning, and a wide eye showing a lot of white is equally to be avoided as it can denote wildness. I like a horse to have a large, prominent eye with a good expression. Small piggy eyes, short thick ears and a prominent forehead, all add up to sulkiness or worse.

You can tell a lot about a horse's character and temperament from his head.

6   Never be taken in when you are told that the horse is really keen. What that probably means is that he pulls like hell, and you will end the day with arms that feel a good inch or two longer than they were when you started, aching shoulders, and in a state of complete exhaustion. A fast horse that pulls often tends to be the slowest in the end, particularly in a country with small enclosures.

7   Never forget that it is blood and action that carry weight, not sheer size. Ill-bred bulk will not carry you all day, and there is a very true saying: 'An ounce of blood is worth a pound of bone'.

8   Above all, it is imperative nowadays that your horse should be completely traffic-proof. Unfortunately only time will tell you this with absolute certainty. Very often horses will be impossible when they meet a tractor out hacking, but do not even notice the very same vehicle when they meet it in the hunting field, as then they have their minds on their work.

For myself, I like to have what could be described as a classy-looking horse and, although there can be no such thing as a bad colour in a horse – there are only good horses and bad horses – I must admit I do not care for a washy chestnut, and have always had a preference for bays or dark browns.

As I like to have plenty in front of me, I look for good sloping shoulders and plenty of front, with the neck and head meeting at an angle of about 90°. Riding pretty heavy as I do, I have to look for plenty of bone, and like a large flat knee that is near to the ground in relation to the length of the leg. I like a horse to have a wide chest with plenty of heart room (though not so wide that the forelegs are too far apart), and plenty of depth with well sprung ribs.

The paces of a horse are very important, for nothing is more tiring or uncomfortable than riding all day on a horse that has an awkward gait. The walk should be long, free and swinging, and I have always found that a horse that strides out well tends to be a good ride, and is likely to be a good galloper – though galloping properly is something a young horse needs to learn to do. The trot must be low, level and straight, and any tendency to too much knee action is a fault. When galloping, the horse should cover as much ground as possible with each stride. However, it is possible for a horse with a good disposition and action to be a brilliant performer even if he appears to be badly built, strange though that may seem in the light of all these comments.

I come back again to what I said at the outset. It is you who are going to ride the horse, and therefore you must try to find one that meets your requirements on as many counts as possible so that you can enjoy happy hunting.

You may put on his clothes; every sportsman, they say,
* In his lifetime has one that outrivals the rest,*
So the pearl of my casket I've shown you to-day,
* The gentlest, the gamest—the boldest, the best;*
And I never will part, by a sale or swop,
With my Clipper that stands in the stall at the top!

G. J. Whyte Melville

18
A Defence of Fox-Hunting

There is no doubt that a fox-hunter is bound to meet at some time in his life a person who will attack his sport, and therefore himself, as being cruel and brutalising. This attack will probably be both vitriolic and uninformed. It will not be enough to maintain a dignified silence, nor will it be wise to enter into what will become a heated argument, unless you have given the matter a good deal of thought and can produce an informed defence.

There is an excellent case for fox-hunting, and I think that it should be put forward with as much vigour as possible, for one antagonist converted could lead to more – though sometimes sadly one has to admit defeat in the face of bigoted determination to see only one point of view.

What I propose now is to put before you some ideas that will provide you with ammunition and which will, I hope, give you cause to think a great deal about the whole subject. You will then be able to form your own opinion, which will be all the more valuable because it will be based on your own personal views and experience.

What we must never forget is that hunting is a very important part of the tradition of our countryside – part of our whole heritage in fact. This is much more so in certain parts of the country than in others, for in some places hunting is almost like a religion, and the people concerned become nearly as bigoted as the 'antis', which undoubtedly lays them open to criticism. I would prefer to say that the love of hunting is undoubtedly a way of life.

The first and the main accusation that is always made is that hunting is cruel. This nearly always emanates from ignorance, and can only be made by people who have not studied the ways of the wild. I would not be foolish enough to state categorically that hunting is never cruel. Unfortunately, not all the people who hunt are humane, and there is no doubt that some cruelty does occur, but these are isolated cases and I am absolutely certain that they do not happen with well-run packs of hounds.

Never let yourself fall into the trap of saying that a fox enjoys being hunted. Of course he does not enjoy it. But if your opponent (for we must call him that) should then go on to ask how you yourself would like to be chased by a pack of dogs, killed and eaten, then you will have him cold. You can turn round straightaway and retort that naturally you would simply loathe it, but fortunately for you you do not happen to be a fox, so you do not have to live in a hole, and you are not obliged to subsist on nasty things like rats, mice, beetles and raw frogs' legs, which would be horrible. But nor do you have to hunt to kill every day of your life for your very existence. You can finish up by saying that you would not particularly enjoy being, let us say for the sake of argument, in the front line of fire during the war, in a bomber, or in a large city that was under attack, or the victim of the violence that abounds in the urban streets these days, or confronted by burglars in your house – but those would amount to conditions of emergency and would therefore be quite different.

It must not be forgotten that the fox's whole subsistence comes from what he himself kills, for that is the basis of his life-style. We too, kill many things for food, it is just that we do not go down to the slaughter house and witness the killing of everything we eat, nor do we do the deed ourselves. Let us hope that your contestant is not a vegetarian, for you will then be forced to change your tactics!

It is, of course, impossible to compare the feelings of a wild animal – or indeed any animal – with those of a human being. The idea of endowing animals with human characteristics, then dressing them up and causing them to play out a drama satirising the faults of men is nothing new, for it has been popular with writers throughout the ages – witness Aesop's fables. I myself dislike those children's books where wild animals are dressed up in clothes, given human feelings and made to talk with human words. The Peter Rabbit books, though undoubtedly full of charm and talent, have been responsible for quite a lot of what I would call silly sentimentality. The only story in which an animal talked that I really enjoyed was one called *Tobermory* by Saki (H. H. Munro). Tobermory was a cat that was taught to speak by some man with weird notions; but once it was able to talk, this sagacious cat turned the tables on the human beings by creeping along the bedroom windowsills each night at a houseparty, and then 'telling' the next morning!

Let us then accept the fact that although children may enjoy such stories, we left the ranks of childhood long ago, and the business of the defence of our sport is a deperately serious issue that requires study and thought.

All animals fear pain, some people believe they fear death, but man is the only one who has the knowledge and imagination that enables him to anticipate it. This is not so with other animals for, even if they can fear death, their fear only becomes a reality when death is imminent; they are not capable of worrying themselves about it beforehand. There is, possibly, occasionally an exception, and you may be sure that it will be trotted out by your opponent in an argument. He will tell you of the bullock that, maddened with fear, escapes from the slaughter-house and runs amok. What is most likely is that its fear has arisen from the smell of blood, and is caused by its instinctive knowledge of the imminence of disaster.

To return to the fox: he is himself a hunter, and is therefore accustomed to every man's hand being against him, and he is also a wild animal and therefore not endowed with imagination, though we know that he is extremely cunning, and is clever to the extreme. He is always being harassed and chased by dogs, so why should he necessarily be more afraid when he hears hounds? I fancy he just looks on them as another of the hazards of life from which he must escape by using all the ingenuity at his command.

I have never been particularly aware of a fox that is being hunted looking more fearful than he does when one catches him in the headlights of the car; and I have several times seen one stop in the middle of a hunt and pounce on a hen or duck, kill it, and then carry it off. Do the opponents of hunting pity the poor poultry, or do they conveniently forget about them? They should go into a hen-house the morning after a fox has paid a nocturnal visit. Although in normal circumstances a fox does not kill just for the sake of killing, but kills for the food it needs, particularly in the case of a vixen with a hungry family or a dog-fox that is helping her in her task, there seems to be something about the confines of a hen-house with its occupants all squawking and cackling with terror, beating their wings and flying violently around, that triggers off a fox into a frenzy of slaughter, and the result is not a pretty sight.

The basic truth, I think, is that a fox is an eternal optimist, and therefore always thinks he is going to escape right up to the moment when he is bowled over by the leading hound and nipped in the neck by the next one.

Although in hunting the odds against the fox may seem to be enormous when you take into account the number of hounds that are pitted against him, in practice it does not work out like that. The Huntsman using all his faculties has to be very skilful indeed at his work if he is going to be successful and kill foxes, for hounds hunt by scent alone – hardly ever by sight. That means that they are put at an immediate disadvantage, for you may be sure that the fox will take every possible opportunity to mask his scent. The presence of the Hunt followers, either mounted, on foot, or in motor-cars, makes not a jot of difference to the fox – indeed they are all too often a decided hindrance to hounds, and therefore in effect become allies of their intended victim.

As likely as not, will come the question, is it not cruel to chase an animal until it drops from exhaustion, and is it not cruel then to tear it alive, limb from limb? Your retort must be quick and to the point. Were these the true facts, then you would have to answer 'yes' to both questions. But the truth is that the fox is not chased until he drops from exhaustion, but chased until the superior speed and stamina of the hounds allow them to overtake him. Even then, he is certainly not torn limb from limb alive – that used to happen at Tyburn to human beings in the good old days! No, he is killed by a bite in the neck from the second hound, after the leading hound has knocked him over, and therefore he is stone dead by the time the rest of the pack can have a go at him. This can be substantiated by looking at the bodies of foxes killed by the Fell packs in and around the Lake District, where the fox is rarely fed to hounds and hardly ever shows marks of violence.

Now we come to the controversial subject of digging. This is cruel, make no bones about it. But it is necessary, and if it is not undertaken by the Hunt under controlled conditions, it would be undertaken by others under a totally opposite set of conditions: one of extreme cruelty and brutality. Better by far to be dug out and either shot cleanly in the head or killed with a sharp blow, than to be smoked or dug out and then clobbered to death with a shovel, or torn to pieces by three or four bloodthirsty terriers.

The next argument that the 'antis' may well produce is that the fox is preserved in order that the foxhunting maniacs may get their pleasure from hunting him. Yes, all right, but the beef or lamb that possibly you are devouring at the moment was also preserved for our edification and enjoyment.

Now it is time to go into the attack. We must tell those humanitarians of the variety of diabolical ways in which a fox would undoubtedly meet his end were there not an efficient Hunt to make sure that he has a sporting chance of getting away to live and breed. In fact, although my job always is to try to kill foxes, I must admit that occasionally I feel that if a really good fox has managed to get away, either by skill or cunning, then that is obviously the right stock for future breeding purposes.

The fox is not a pretty red furry animal with a lovely bushy tail, he is a killer of lambs and chickens and a real menace to a struggling farmer, especially one who farms in the less wealthy regions of the British Isles. We will not allow the old argument to be trotted out that 'nothing is ever right' for the farmer. Let the townsman rise at five o'clock every morning – every morning of the year – to milk a herd of cows that first he has to muck out and wash off, often struggling with elements that would in other circumstances send him scuttling to the fireside or to the nearest pub. Let the townsman finish his day by going out, whatever the weather, to feed his stock and have a last look round before he can go to bed and seek his well-earned rest.

Traditionally the farmer makes the Hunt welcome, but the farmer is also a realist and he must be satisfied that in the long run, over a season, it is worth his while either from the business point of view or, far more often, because he himself is a lover of hunting and hounds. Undoubtedly, without the goodwill of the farmers, there could not and would not be any hunting.

The trap or snare is the most common and perhaps the most effective means that would-be fox killers use. But a fox in a trap may linger there for days, when he will be suffering the torments of a broken or torn limb, as well as all the terror felt by a wild animal when it is enclosed in any way. Some foxes have been known to gnaw right through their leg in order to free themselves, then make off with a bleeding raw stump to suffer an even slower and more painful death. It is not a pretty thought.

When it comes to the use of a shot-gun, it must always be remembered that any shot at a fox is bound to be a 'chance' one. The fox is not going to walk up and put himself in a position where it is possible to shoot him simply and cleanly. He will present a rapidly moving and twisting target and the chances are that any shot that actually hits him will not kill him outright, but cause dreadful wounds. That poor fox will undoubtedly die of gangrene, because foxes and rats do not lick their wounds and thus cleanse them like other animals. I think I would far rather be hunted and killed outright than die of a gangrenous stomach. What a mercy it is that we do not have to face the choice.

Now let us think of poison. If you have ever seen the look on an animal's face when it has been poisoned it is a memory that will always live with you. Let us then rule out poison as a barbarous means of despatch.

Does the fox, in fact, need to be controlled? Could he not continue and be made a protected species, and what would be his end if that were to happen? An individual fox would go on for perhaps eight or nine years, for foxes are not very long-lived, and eventually he would find himself unable to hunt. As advancing age made it impossible for him to catch the food necessary for his survival, he would then gradually starve to death. If the fox species became too numerous, food would become scarcer, and natural culling would take place through the same slow starvation and disease.

There does not seem to me to be any choice over what is by far the most humane method of dealing with a pest. After all, you do not hear the townsman carrying on over the methods used to exterminate rats. When they put in an appearance in urban streets, perhaps as a result of a dustman's strike, no methods are objected to on the grounds that they are too cruel or inhumane – all that is required is that they should be removed immediately by whatever methods will prove swift and efficacious.

Now let us take a look at the people who hunt the fox. Fox-hunting is in fact a democratic sport enjoyed by the masses, though I doubt whether you will get far if you try to put that point over to the prejudiced, especially in the fashionable Countries. To them, all those expensively dressed people mounted on extremely valuable animals seem to give the lie to that argument. What they do not realise and, moreover, do not want to admit, is that there are many, many more people all over the country who manage to hunt on a shoestring, and as many again who enjoy a day out with hounds in the car or on foot.

If you have taken in what you have earlier read in this book, then you will have many arguments at your fingertips. Fox-hunting after all is a very unselfish sport requiring a great deal of teamwork and it calls for real physical courage, and produces physical fitness of a high degree. Does it really matter that it is a sport that is shared and enjoyed by the wealthiest in the land as well as the poorest? Rich and poor alike stay in the cold and damp, getting frozen to their saddles by choice, in order that they may enjoy this fine sport.

We people who hunt for pleasure and for the sport are not monsters of sadism and iniquity, far from it. If you take a look at the statistics, you will find that the vast majority of Hunt subscribers

"That's something I've wanted all my life—a chance to give a foxhound a nip in the buttocks."

Giles's sense of humour rises to the occasion

also subscribe to an animal charity or some other organisation formed for the preservation of wild life and many are active members of such societies. Most of them have high moral standards and take a part in church, village and country affairs, sit on local magistrates' benches, school and hospital committees and are generally concerned about the well-being of others.

Until quite recent times, and even nowadays in some places, the horse has undoubtedly been a symbol of wealth and power, and in bygone ages the horseman was thought of as an oppressor. It may in fact be a hangover from those times that causes some of the feeling of antagonism that is undoubtedly felt towards the mounted field.

Does it really matter if a man wears what to the townsman appear to be strange clothes? The clothes worn by a man in the hunting field have evolved in the main for utilitarian purposes and the colour of his coat is from that point of view immaterial. What matters is that it

I often break my holiday, which I always spend in Scotland, to judge at a puppy show

is made of strong durable stuff that will keep out the wind and the rain, having all sorts of little waterproof interlinings, and pockets, flaps and buttons that serve a purpose and keep the wearer as warm and dry as circumstances can permit. The hat, which may be a tall silk one, a bowler or a hunting cap, is designed to stop the falling rider from breaking his skull. The hunting tie will act as a splint in case of neck injuries, and it also prevents the rain from pouring down the rider's neck. The leather boots are intended to prevent leg injuries, and the whip is not a weapon – the end with the thong is used to keep hounds away from a horse's heels and thus prevent them from being kicked, its horn handle is for opening and shutting gates, and very often for a multitude of other purposes when the hand alone would not have sufficient strength.

Nobody complains about people wearing white for cricket and tennis as that has proved to be the best colour for summer conditions. The long peaked cricket cap is worn to keep the sun out of the batsman's eyes, and nowadays top-class cricketers wear helmets with visors for exactly the same reason as the hat is worn by the followers of hounds – to prevent head injuries. The pads protect the batsman's and wicketkeeper's legs in the same way as the hunting-boots.

To my mind, anybody is welcome to spend his money in whatever way that will give him the most pleasure. Should he prefer to lay out large sums on a winter cruise, to provide his surburban home with a heated swimming pool, or to drive a high-powered car, who am I to criticise? I myself, in common with many other thousands of sportsmen, happen to choose to spend all my spare cash on my hounds and my hunting, and I do not really care whether I wear old clothes – many of my suits date back a good many years, I am still wearing pre-war shoes and most of the brief holidays I take generally include quite a bit of business concerned with hunting, perhaps taking in judging at a puppy show on my way to Scotland for a few days' salmon fishing. I think if you were to question most Masters of Hounds, you would get much the same answer, and very many of them nowadays are working farmers.

Everyone is made welcome in the hunting field by the officials of the Hunt, the only provisos being that he must pay his way and keep to the rules.

Hunting provides a living for great numbers of people on the perimeter of the sport, and they are not doing their work in the main for the good of fox-hunting any more than the people who manufacture alchoholic drink or tobacco are doing that solely either to benefit mankind by the solace that such products undoubtedly bring to certain sections of humanity, or to cause the consumers of their products to suffer from an early death. They are all in it for the money.

I would like to mention a few of the people who directly or indirectly make their living from hunting. First there is the man who breeds the horses. Then there is the man who produces the food they eat; not 'the man' but many thousands of men by the time the oats and bran appear in the horse's manger, the hay in his net and the straw on the floor of his box. Next there come the manufacturers and sellers of the saddlery, all the veterinary products for horses and for hounds, and the clothing. This list could go on almost indefinitely before ever we come to the people who are actually employed by the Hunts. There are many groups that could be said to have 'fringe benefits' from hunting, such as riding schools that teach people the basic arts of horsemanship and hotels that benefit from the extra custom brought by visiting sportsmen, to say nothing of the pubs and restaurants. What a mass of unemployment would follow should hunting cease, especially in those areas where it can be classed as amounting almost to a major industry.

Now we come to the transport. Many lorries that are used to take the horses on to the meet on Mondays, are also used to take cattle to market on Fridays, and for a multitude of other purposes round a farm on the other days of the week. The same thing applies to the Land Rovers and other vehicles that draw horse-trailers.

Do not let yourself be drawn by the argument that the Hunt invades the privacy of the individual. The truth is that the Hunt only goes where it is invited and welcome, and does not set foot on land where it is unwelcome except, of course, in exceptional or accidental circumstances. There are always stories being bandied about, especially in a certain type of newspaper that thrives on such tales that can lead to controversial correspondence, of kills taking place in surburban front gardens. These are rare occurrences and to be deplored.

It is true that hunting does hold up the traffic, but not very often, and not very widely, and never in town or city centres. Processions, funerals and weddings tend to be far worse offenders!

A foxhound is far less savage than that common domestic pet, the cat, which is one of the most diabolically cruel members of the animal species in the way in which it terrorises its prey before going in to the kill. It is a sadistic, slow killer, whereas a foxhound puts an end to its prey with one snap of the jaw.

In conclusion, I would like to say that I feel very strongly that there is an invaluable personal discipline in hunting, specially when it is properly imbibed in early childhood. Human beings do have latent aggressive tendencies that in ancient times were satisfied by war and the constant need for self-defence and preservation. Better surely that those tendencies should be directed into a sport that is so exhilarating and carries with it goodwill and comradeship of the best kind, than that it should vent itself in soccer hooliganism and the sort of violence that makes the streets of our cities unsafe for both young and old.

19
First-aid for Horse and Rider

First-aid in the hunting field can only be a matter of emergency treatment in the light of the materials to hand, and therefore can only be of a very elementary nature.

However, it is a good thing to be aware – though not, I trust, to anticipate – that accidents do happen, and that it may be necessary for you yourself to do something to help. Indeed, you may find yourself alone at the scene of the accident and be obliged to use your ingenuity to deal with the situation.

Bandages have to be improvised from handkerchiefs, braces, neckties or any piece of cloth that may be available, and a tourniquet can be made with a clean handkerchief folded to make a hard pad, which can then be bound on as tightly as possible with a tie. Extra pressure can be applied by using a piece of stick to twist and tighten this improvised bandage.

A very tired horse may have a bad fall in some small place merely because he is exhausted. It will then be necessary to remove his saddle, make him as comfortable as possible, and let him rest to regain his wind. After ten minutes or so he may be able to rise with no help, but should he not do so the rider if all right should take the reins, and one man should pull the forelegs out in front of the horse when he has been propped up on his breast. Then a man should be placed on either side to steady the horse, with another man or two by his tail, to help to raise the hindquarters. Once on his feet, the horse should be allowed to rest for another ten or fifteen minutes and then, if he can walk, he should be taken slowly and gently to the nearest farm.

The following passage from David Brock's *The Foxhunter's Week-end Book,* although very funny, also contains some thoroughly practical advice:

Broken Back: Every fox-hunter, worth his salt, has experienced the sensation of arriving in a deep ditch with the inverted horse above him, and, after having been extricated and laid reverently upon a gate prior to removal to the mortuary, of wondering whether his horse's back is broken. For a horse in such a position realises that it looks a trifle stupid, and thinks, by feigning mortal injury, to obtain sympathy rather than jibe. He can really get in the most embarrassing positions and suffer no hurt, yet break his back from an innocent-seeming fall. To make up your mind whether the back is broken:

1   If you can find it at the bottom of the ditch, pick up the tail; if it is lifeless, fear the worst.
2   Remove a non-essential pin from your person and apply it forcibly to a hind limb; if the horse kicks or flinches all is well.

The next thing is to extract the horse from the ditch: this requires the assistance of nine other fox-hunters, glad of a chance to escape with dignity from the task of facing other, possibly deeper, ditches ahead, and a minimum of fourteen agricultural labourers, one horse-dealer, one farmer, the village postman, four small urchins, five smaller urchines, one massive amazon, and a small and insignificant second horseman, obviously a fool. After you have listened to the advice of the fox-hunters (and in the process have got the horse more firmly embedded in the ditch) and of the yokels (and you have broken the tree of the saddle and permanently lent your knife), and after you have been told by the urchins that you have a muddy back and by the urchines that the last horse in that ditch was never no more good a'terwards, mister, and by the buxom wench that the pore animal is dead; after the farmer has sent the horse-breaker for ropes and a plough team (and, in Ireland, has haggled with you for the price) one of two things will happen:

1   The horse may extract itself with one large grunt, treading on your hat in the process, or
2   The insignificant second-horseman will, with no effort, extract it unaided for you.

Should your horse appear to have a broken back, on no account move him until a veterinary surgeon has seen him, because he will be in no pain if the back is in fact broken, and if it is not it may be possible to cure him.

Every now and then in the hunting field you will have reason to wonder whether your horse is sound. If you think he is not, his lameness may be caused by a variety of things; bruised or rubbed joints, sprains of the tendons, or stones jammed in the feet are the usual causes. If after removing any obvious cause, the horse is still lame, you will have to take him home and call the veterinary surgeon. The latter will find it a great help if you are able more or less to pin-point the time that the horse showed signs of lameness, ie after a fence with a big drop, or after landing on soft, sticky ground, or on a hard road.

If your horse starts to sweat and breathe heavily at the end of a run, you should suspect congestion of the lung. Get off and loosen the girths, then turn his head into the wind. He should then be taken to the nearest farm, and no attempt should be made to move him again until his breathing has been normal for at least two hours.

Your horse may suffer from a spasm of the diaphragm after a very fast run, and this is often mistaken for heart trouble, as it may be possible to hear a dull, thumping sound from some distance away that sounds awful. The best emergency treatment for this condition is a tumblerful of whisky mixed with an equal amount of water, after which he should be walked quietly home or to his box.

Bleeding from the nostrils is alarming, and is sometimes the result of a fall. However it often happens for no explicable reason with highly bred hunters after severe exertion, and is frequently found to be an inherited trait. If the horse is taken to a quiet place, the bleeding may stop quickly of its own accord. If it continues, then apply cold water to the forehead and face. When the bleeding has stopped, it would be wise to rest the horse for an hour or two before taking him home.

If your horse gets cast in a bog, and shows no signs of getting up, fill your hat with water and pour it in his ear. You will be amazed at his immediate reaction, and many a horse's life has been saved this way in countries where soft ground is common.

Useful adjuncts to your hunting equipment, and which will not detract seriously from your general sartorial elegance, are a puffer spray of antiseptic powder and a compressed wound dressing consisting of a sterile pad of cotton wool attached to a bandage. In the old days of silver coins, most people always carried a half-crown to use with a tourniquet, but now you will have to use your ingenuity in seeking a substitute.

There may be a moment when you discover your horse is injured. First of all, someone will shout over his shoulder as he gallops past: 'You know your horse is bleeding from X Y Z, don't you?' If you didn't, you will not be in ignorance for long, because you will be provided with the information by the next half-dozen galloping horsemen, and then ten to one you will be left all alone to cope as best you can. Your horse will be wanting to go on and you will know you must not, and so he will be rushing round in circles. Although blood is pouring from X Y Z, the mud will be so thick that you will be unable to see whether it is in fact from X, Y or Z. First you must try to find some water and wash off the mud so that you can see exactly where the injury is and also its extent.

Half the injuries out hunting are caused by over-reaching. If the wound is a shallow one on the horse's coronet, puff some antiseptic on it, remount and try to catch up. If however the cut is deep, put in the antiseptic and then apply your bandage as tightly as you can. If you apply this bandage tightly enough, the bleeding will stop, and you can walk the horse back to his box or to a nearby farm where you can leave him while you fetch the box. If he tends to over-reach, it is a good idea to have the inside edge of the hind shoes rounded and set back as far as possible.

If your horse has struck a tendon, start the bandage at the lower end of the flap of skin and work upwards. If the bleeding does not stop, put a tourniquet above the seat of the injury, but on no account move the horse more than you must.

All you can do with bad tears is to try to stop the bleeding and call for the assistance of a veterinary surgeon as quickly as possible. There are three things that you can do in an emergency:

1 Put on a tight bandage
2 Plug the wound with cotton wool
3 Apply a tourniquet above the wound

Always keep the horse quiet for half an hour after the bleeding has stopped, or it may start again and be even worse and more difficult to staunch.

Should you be unfortunate enough to break your horse's knees on jumping into a road, bathe them with cold water, but do not try to pick out the pieces of stone for you may end up by opening the joint. After bathing, apply antiseptic.

Now we come to first-aid for the human species. While I do not suggest that you employ an ambulance to follow you about, people have been known to come home from hunting on a hurdle as an improvised stretcher, myself among them. I do urge you to attend a course of first-aid lectures; you will find them invaluable.

One of the most common hunting accidents is a fracture,

especially of the arm and collar bone. If there is a break, usually the patient will feel no pain for a time, and there is none of the swelling or deformity that is caused by a sprain. No attempt should be made to set a fracture. For a broken arm, leave the rider's coat on, for its thickness will act as padding, then put on a splint over the coat, the arm being bent to a right angle; a rolled newspaper or piece of cardboard can be used, secured by three folded handkerchiefs over the seat of the fracture. A sling can be made out of a large silk handkerchief which somebody is bound to be carrying. A drop of whisky *as long as the patient is not concussed* is a good idea.

If you suspect a broken collar bone, do not remove the coat, but place the arm in a sling then bind a long folded handkerchief, or whatever is to hand, right round the injured arm and the sound arm at the armpit level, and tie it at the back, bracing back both shoulders. The comfort of a sling always depends on the arm being supported from wrist to elbow.

Fractured legs are best left entirely to a doctor, so leave the patient on the ground, putting your coat under his head as a pillow, and send for help. Do not attempt to take off the boot, which will act as a splint. If it does have to be cut off, try to do this down the back seam, bearing in mind the price of new ones.

If there are fractured ribs, the breathing will become laboured and terrifyingly bright and frothy blood may be coughed up. You must try to make the patient comfortable by tying two broad pieces of material round the chest, slightly overlapping each other and knotting each at the far side. Under no circumstances should a stimulant be given, though hot sweet tea or coffee and a cigarette which help alleviate the effects of shock may be offered.

Dislocations should be left well alone for skilled assistance and treatment.

When you suspect concussion, keep the patient as quiet as possible, and if at all feasible, apply a cold compress at the back of the neck. Again, under no circumstances should a stimulant be given.

Should you have to resort to transporting the patient on a hurdle, let the progress be slow and gentle, and if possible provide some sort of padding such as a coat or a sack stuffed with hay or straw.

Should you have no disinfectant for an open wound, a drop of whisky will act as a substitute. By the way, a tot of whisky poured down the boot is a wonderful foot warmer – in other words, pour it down your own throat, and it will reach your feet in double quick time!

Princess Anne, the first member of the present Royal Family to wear the Blue and Buff

20

Etiquette and Clothes

Etiquette – taken from *The Ten Commandments of Fox-hunting by Mr Young* (written about the time I was born)

Article I Every man shall present himself at the place of meeting quietly, suitably clothed, and in good time. He who rides his hunter steadily thereto is better than he who uses a hack. He who drives tandem for display or who uses any manner of engine or machine, except as a necessity, is an abomination.

Article II Every man shall first salute and speak words of comfort to the hunstman and whippers-in, knowing full well that they have hard work to perform. He shall then count the hounds and examine them with great joy, but in a quiet manner. He shall likewise cheerfully salute his friends. He that shall say the day will be a bad-scenting one, or in any manner endeavour to prophesy evil, is an abomination.

Article III It is acceptable that those of experience shall, at all times, give explanation and encouragement by word and deed to all young persons, so that fox-hunting may continue in the land from generation to generation. He who thinks he knows, when he knows not, is an abomination.

Article IV Every man shall remember that the ground he passes over is not his own property. Whosoever uses not due care and consideration is an abomination.

Article V He who talks loudly or who leaps unnecessarily is an abomination. He who wears an apron or mackintosh on wet days or who uses any other device for making a mountebank of himself, or who in any way causes inconvenience to any hound or hunt servant is an abomination.

Article VI   If it be possible, let every true believer abstain from all meat and drink, save only such as is necessary to sustain life. Let the whole day be kept as a special fasting and strengthening of the mind for the Chase. In the evening he shall partake of suitable meat and drink, and on the evening after a good day he shall have a special allowance.

Article VII   He who, of his own free will, goes home before the hounds do, or who is displeased with the day, or who is not fully uplifted, joyful and thankful because of the day, is an abomination.

Article VIII   Whosoever kills or takes a fox by any other means save by hunting is an abomination; his dwelling shall become desolate and his possessions a desert; may his mind be filled with bitterness and his body with pain.

Article IX   Whosoever lives a cheerful, good neighbour, striving to help and encourage his friends at all times, and who hunts on foot if he has not a horse, and by whose behaviour the Scarlet is never brought into dishonour; may he live long, and be happy and may his possessions be as the sand by the sea-shore for multitude.

Article X   And may all men, rich and poor, have equal rights and pleasures in the Chase if they devoutly agree to these articles.

Clothes

Fashion is not very rife in the hunting field – tradition seems to be the thing – though in the early days at Peterborough I understand that the huntsmen wore long tops and their coats came down to their ankles. Caps were worn as a regular thing until the Marquess of Waterford broke his neck in 1859 when wearing one, and then people took to silk hats, and to bowler hats when they became fashionable towards the end of Queen Victoria's reign. That people were swayed by strange things is indicated by the fact that they gave up wearing black velvet because Mrs Manning, the notorious murderess, was hanged in a black velvet gown in 1849!

It is not known for certain why the red coat became *de rigueur*, though my own green derives from the colours of the family livery, as does the Berkeley yellow.

The two buttons at the back of the huntsman's coat serve as a reminder of the sword belt, and the buttons below were for the looping up of the garment when the lanes were muddy and foul.

The cut of a red coat is important. It should have a fairly long opening at the neck with two buttons and a hook and eye where the third button should come, well-rounded points in front and not be straight cut like a hunt servant's. The back should be lined with flannel and it should have two side pockets with flaps set at an angle on the skirts. Make sure that the back is really well lined, as that is where the cold strikes hardest. On the way home you will find that newspaper is a wonderfully simple way of restoring heat to the body.

White breeches should be worn with a red coat, either made of cotton or cavalry twill which, although more difficult to clean, is the more durable material. Nowadays there are new materials on the market which are extremely serviceable in that not only are they very easy to clean, but they fit of their own accord, stretching to mould the contours of the body. These 'stretch breeches' have been adopted by most of the younger people who hunt.

The waistcoat may be of yellow or checked material, although some people elect to wear a white one. Again it should be well lined for the same reasons as for the coat, and the pockets should be made with flaps to prevent your loose change from flying out.

Boots should be of black leather, though nowadays there are excellent rubber ones on the market which for reasons of economy and because they are so easy to clean, have been adopted by very many people. I personally am of the opinion that although they certainly have their merits, they are not nearly as safe as leather, as they do not offer anything like the same protection to the legs. Also it is often necessary to use irons a size or two smaller than normal because rubber boots are narrow and the soles tend to slip when they get wet. Boots should have light tops, though here again brown ones have been adopted by many people because they are easier to clean. The boot garters should be white if white breeches are being worn. Their tongues should go outwards and they should fix between the third and fourth buttons of the breeches. For some reason three buttons should be shown for leggings and four for boots.

Leather boots must be thick soled, as not only will they be much warmer, but you will find them much easier to get off at the end of the day. There should be a spur rest just above the instep.

It is interesting to read that Beau Brummell (1778–1840) designed the modern hunting boot; before he entered the hunting field, pictures and caricatures showed baggy long-topped boots with broad garters coming above the knee. Brummell's boots always had white tops, and these always used to be the correct wear. He told an admiring enquirer that the wonderful polish on his boots came from using blacking mixed with peaches and champagne! Certainly many people used white of egg to get a lustre on their boots which made them look like patent leather.

Beau Brummell, although not noted for being a wise man, was

however wise enough to say that the best-dressed man in the hunting field was the man whose dress attracted least notice.

On the question of spurs, a lot of people think that they are a necessary part of hunting wear, but it all depends on how they are to be used and also on the horse you are riding. So do not let yourself be influenced too much by others, do what you yourself think right.

Black coats should be cut on the same line as red ones, with black or black-engraved hunt buttons, but the breeches should be buff or yellow. If you wear white breeches with a dark or dark-grey coat, you should wear light coloured tops. With other breeches the tops should be of patent leather, and a silk hat should be worn.

It is entirely a matter of personal choice whether you choose a cut-away or swallow-tailed coat in either colour.

The following story I am assured is true. Two sportsmen once went to hunt in Ireland with the Meath, where there are so many banks and ditches of such proportions that men known as 'wreckers' stand on top waiting to collect half-crowns for rescue work. Both these hunters were beautifully turned out, and would have graced Beau Brummell's company. Their hats gleamed, their coats looked as if they had been painted on them like those of toy soldiers, their leathers looked as if they had just come from the tailor's, and you could have seen to shave in the shine of their boots – and to crown it all, both of them wore exquisite bunches of Parma violets in their buttonholes. Sad to say, both came to grief in the same ditch.

Said Pat to Mike, 'What have ye there, Mike?'

Mike said he wasn't sure, but he thought it was 'a rider and his harse'.

After some of the clinging mud had been scraped off, and both the sportsmen were standing on dry ground once more, Pat exclaimed:

'Begorra, Mike, it is no man at all, at all: sure, they're a couple of paycocks!'

Always bear in mind Egerton Warburton's famous poem:

> T'aint the red coat makes the rider
> Leathers, boots nor yet the cap.
>
> They who come their coats to show, they
> Better were at home in bed;
> What of hounds and hunting know they?
> Nothing else but 'go ahead';
> At the Kennel I could train 'em
> If they would but come to school,
> Two and two in couples chain 'em,
> Feed on meal, and keep 'em cool.

My mother, a picture of sartorial elegance, riding 'The Goat', a horse that also carried King George V when he was Prince of Wales and Field Marshal Earl Roberts VC

Some Further Points

The Red Coat Dress (please, not 'pink', though scarlet is acceptable)

Headgear: a silk hat is, I think, probably the safest headgear, though I am happy for the lady members of my Field to wear hunting caps. This is normally the prerogative of ex-Masters of Hounds and of farmers and their wives. By and large, very many ladies nowadays wear caps when they have obtained permission from their Master of Hounds to do so. The ribbons at the back should be sewn up – I know not why – as to leave them dangling is to denote that you are an official or a member of the hunt staff. A hat-guard should not be worn, as not only is it always thought to be the sign of a cad – again I do not know why – but it certainly prevents the hat from being taken off to signal which way a fox has gone.

A plain white hunting tie, which I was brought up to call a tie and not a 'stock'. To me a stock is part of a gun; goods in a shop; or, my lady friends tell me, something that is used to make soup. It also, of course, denotes sheep or cows. Please make sure that you learn to tie it neatly and correctly. Most are sold nowadays with easy-to-follow instructions, but the tying soon becomes second nature. Be sure to secure the first knot with a safety pin from underneath, and also pin down the ends where they do not show very securely. Nothing looks worse than a flapping tie.

A plain, gold horizontal tie-pin should be used to secure your tie, unless you belong to a Hunt that has its own pin. If worn vertically, it could run into your throat.

A hunting waistcoat: either yellow, checked or occasionally white. This should be worn with the bottom button left unfastened, as with an ordinary waistcoat.

A red coat.

A pair of white breeches with a red coat.

A pair of white garter-straps with white breeches.

A pair of top-boots, which should be black with mahogany tops. With my Hunt it is traditional to have pink tops with Blue and Buff.

A pair of spurs, if you think them necessary. Do not be driven by convention to wear them if you do not feel your horse needs them or, indeed, if you think you would be safer without.

A pair of gloves, which should be white, pale yellow or tan leather, wool or string. It is a wise provision to carry a spare pair under your girth in wet weather.

All the above notes also apply to a black coat, though nowadays ladies tend to wear navy-blue coats with navy-blue caps, and skintight yellow breeches. These latter look very smart, always providing the shape underneath is suitable! Ladies wear butcher boots, ie boots without coloured tops.

The Rat-catcher's Garb

This is the name given to dress worn before 1 November when cub-hunting, and after 1 March. Some members of staghunting packs wear it all the time, though some change into black coats for hind-hunting from November to mid-February. A silk hat is out of place and tends to look downright ridiculous in a Moorland setting and, traditionally there, no one but the Master and hunt staff wear red coats. It consists of:

A bowler hat, or velvet cap.

A collar and tie, or a spotted or pale-blue four-fold silk tie. A white hunting tie is permissible.

A hunting waistcoat.

A tweed riding-coat of suitable weight according to the weather and the time of year.

A pair of buff breeches.

A pair of brown field-boots or black butcher boots.
A pair of brown or black garter-straps according to the colour of
your boots.
A pair of spurs, if you think them necessary.
A pair of gloves.

Now let us have a check on our pockets:
A handkerchief (take a clean white one if you are hunting with a
Moorland pack, as it will show up when held to one side to denote
which way the fox has gone).
A knife with a strong cutting blade that is easy to open, and with a
spike so that a hole may be made in leather to effect a running
repair. Also it really can be used to take stones out of a horse's shoe!
A leather bootlace and a piece of binder twine, which you will find
useful for all sorts of things, tying up gates, repairs to saddlery,
and so on.
Disinfectant in a puffer-spray bottle.
Tourniquet bandage dressing.
Money (loose change – make sure you have the right denomination
so that you may make an emergency telephone call – tied up in
the corner of a handkerchief so that it does not jingle.
Safety pins.
(For ladies) – hair pins and spare hair nets.
Keys – though I think it is wisest to leave them hidden either in or
about your vehicle.
Sustenance – do not forget that many a rib or worse has been broken
by coming in contact with a steel flask.
Your name and address with a telephone number on a card.
If you stay away, paste a comprehensive list of all the things you are
going to need inside the lid of the suitcase that you habitually use.
Everyone's needs vary, but the following list which does not pretend
to be complete, may be found useful when compiling your own:
Boot-hooks or pullers
Jockeys, if used
Put your own boot-jack in the back of your car or horse-box, as
nobody else's is ever really adequate, and can cause a rapid rise in
blood pressure at the end of a day when your feet are maybe wet
either with water or sweat, and will have swelled in any case.
Hunting tights
Warm socks
Spare hunting ties, breeches, shirts and waistcoat just in case you are
invited to stay on for a further day's hunting

Coat

Hat or cap

Button-stock for brass buttons on red coat, and a cleaning pad

Boots complete with trees

Provide yourself with two canvas boot-bags and elastic covers for
your boot tops, so that brown tops will not come into contact
with black boot polish.

Refreshment: Although I know there is a school of thought that
reckons that a hunting day should be a day of starvation, I myself
always carry some sandwiches wrapped in an easily squashed paper,
so that I can shove them back into my pocket as hounds find, which
they invariably do, the moment one's thoughts turn to food. I have
heard it said that the ideal package of sandwiches should be capable
of being opened by one numbed, gloved hand without being
removed from the pocket. Again I turn to David Brock:

> Hunting sandwiches differ from all other sandwiches in that they
> are eaten under vastly more rigorous conditions, and they should
> be prepared with that in view. They should be so cut, formed, and
> packed that they can be enjoyed even though eaten upon the back
> of a runaway mustang, in a hurricane of wind and cold rain, by a
> man who has recently broken his right wrist.

I personally tend to rely on car followers for a drink, for a saddle
flask is invariably made of glass, tends to be slippery, and is generally
irreplaceable. I do wish they could be made aware of the desperation
they arouse in the breasts of the mounted followers as they stand by
their cars downing mugfuls of coffee when conditions are icy, and
lovely refreshing cool drinks when the sun is shining. I myself am
generally too busy to worry about it, but I must say I am very thankful when someone comes up and offers me a short drink at the end of
an arduous run and, more particularly, a cup of tea at the end of the
day before our horses' heads are turned for home.

Appendix A: Noises Off

It is almost impossible, I find, to describe on paper the various sounds that you will hear in the hunting field, but they can readily be divided into three different kinds: those made by the human voice, those made by hounds, and those made by the horn. To add to the difficulties, all human voices are different, all hounds make individual noises, and everyone blows a hunting horn differently.

The human voice is used in various ways. It is encouraging when trying to make hounds do something on which they are not particularly keen, such as swim a swollen river or plunge into a deep, thorny covert. It has to be soothing when it is evident that excited nerves must be calmed, and hounds lulled into trying once more for an elusive scent. It has to be used harshly when necessary; but pleasantly when hounds deserve praise. Lastly, it can be exultant as hounds break up their prey.

Hound utterances really are almost impossible to explain, for it takes a lifetime of experience to translate certain woofing noises. By and large, single woofs mean that a fox is on foot; a multitude of woofs is the sound for which everyone has been waiting, and means that hounds are beginning to run. Short, angry, stationary woofs are generally the signal of a hound that is at a loss. Squeaks are to be deplored, as they often denote that a rabbit and not a fox is on foot, while full-blooded shrieks mean trouble of some sort – probably a hound caught up in a fence. There is a subtle change in the cry of the whole pack as they draw near to their prey, which has to be heard as it is impossible to describe. There is also a particular noise that means that hounds are hunting heel-line. This again defies description, and to translate it is a matter of experience.

The horn is used not only to give instructions to hounds and hunt staff, but also to give information to the Field. Again, it can be used in several different ways. It can be used tootingly, as a signal to inform everyone that the Huntsman is still in covert. As explained earlier, when that toot is doubled, it means that the Huntsman is likely to be in some sort of trouble and wants immediate assistance. A screech denotes that a hound has done something wrong, and when it is used wailingly it means that the Huntsman has decided to draw another covert and wants his hounds. It can also mean that he is tired and has decided to go home. When it is used thrillingly, you may be sure that you are in for a gallop.

The actual words that issue from the Huntsman's throat naturally vary not only according to his usual style of speaking and general accent, but also to his degree of freshness or fatigue. I can give you a list, but you really will need to hear them for yourself:

Eleu in there, my lads! Eu in then, little bitches Loo in	All these mean get into that covert and look for a fox
Hike-hike-hike-hike-hike to Merryman-hike! (Hike in this instance means 'hark')	This means that Merryman has found a fox, and all you others must go and join him
Forrard, forrard, forrard-on	Go on as fast as you can
'Old 'ard	Stop in your tracks, usually addressed to pushing members of the Field
Y-ert . . . y-ert . . . y-ert (spoken softly)	A soothing noise intended for anyone whose nerves require it
Who-oop! Who-oop! Who-oop! (generally accompanied by many bloodthirsty expressions)	This denotes that hounds have killed the fox
'Ware – followed by a specific word (pronounced *war*, and meaning 'beware')	Used as a warning from a riot on a hare to a nasty hole or piece of wire.

Bike means 'back' and is one of the first words that a hound needs to learn.

It is truly only practice in this case that will make perfect, and a fox-hunter will find that if he takes an interest he will soon distinguish the excited staccato yapping of young hounds bouncing after bunny-rabbits from the muffled roar of a pack of experienced dog-hounds on the line of a fox. There is a difference between the deep baying of hounds marking a fox and the angry noises they make when they are baying a badger. The cry of hounds running under trees is different from that of hounds running in covert. And a hound caught up in wire emits a shriek that is totally different from the one he lets out when receiving a justified corporal punishment for some offence.

Appendix B: Glossary

All on!

A pack is said to be 'all on' when all the hounds are there. When leaving a covert and at the end of the day, a Whipper-in should count ('make') the pack, and if all are there he reports 'All on, Sir!' If some are still missing, he says perhaps, 'Want a couple and a half, Sir!'

Artificial earth

A refuge for foxes made by a Hunt, with the object of encouraging foxes to breed in a certain part of the country.

Babble

When a hound throws its tongue unnecessarily, for example when it is a long way behind the leading hounds or when it does not have the line of a fox. This tends to mislead both the Huntsman and the rest of the pack.

Back at the knee

A fault in conformation of both hounds and horses. When seen from the side, the knee and fore-arm appear to be behind the vertical level of the lower leg.

Back, To

To back a horse is to ride it for the first time; as well as to put a wager on it.

Bag-fox

A bag-fox, or bagged-fox, or 'bagman', is a fox which is turned out of a sack, enclosure or drain into which he has previously been put, in order that he may be hunted.

Ball

An equine pill. To ball-up is when snow clogs in a horse's hooves making it seem to be on slippery stilts.

Bars

The fleshy ridges on the upper part of a horse's mouth.

Bay

Hounds marking a fox to ground are said to bay. If a stag faces his pursuers, he is at bay, and hounds barking defiance are said to be baying him. A terrier facing a fox or badger

underground and giving tongue is also said to be baying.

Bay

The name given to a rich-brown colour in a horse.

Bedding

Straw, shavings or peat, on which horses or hounds lie when they are resting.

Belvoir tan

A foxhound colour which was very fashionable at one time. The hound is a very dark, rich tan or mahogany, with black markings on the body, but no white above the elbows other than possibly a white collar.

Benches

The platforms upon which hounds sleep in kennels.

Billett

A fox's droppings.

Binder

The horizontal top, thin branch of a cut-and-laid fence (qv). Binder twine ties up bales of hay and straw and, carried in a pocket, is useful in many ways.

Bit

A piece of steel, or often nowadays synthetic material, placed in a horse's mouth in the fond hope that the rider may thereby control his mount. 'Bit' used in conjunction with the words 'and bridoon' means a curb-bit (qv).

Blank

A covert is blank when it does not hold a fox. A blank day is one on which no fox is found.

Blind

A fence is blind when the exact edge of the ditch facing it, or the outline of the bank, is hidden by grass etc. A country is said to be blind when there is still much leaf and old grass about the fences. A jump is taken blind when the hedges are still full of summer leaf and the ditches are overgrown.

Blood

Contrary to the belief of many anti-hunting enthusiasts, who imagine only small children with bloody faces, this expression is also used in connection with hounds. It means giving young hounds their first kill.

A pack which is 'out of blood' is one that has not killed a fox for some time; while one that is 'in blood' has recently killed several foxes in quick succession.

Blood horse

A thoroughbred.

Blowing away

A Huntsman will blow his hounds away from a covert with quick, pulsating notes on his horn, on to the line of a fox. So 'blowing away' is the prelude to a hunt in the open.

Blowing out

A Huntsman will blow his hounds out of a blank covert with long mournful wails on his horn.

Bob-tailed

A bob-tailed fox is one either without a brush at all, or with a very short brush, generally the result of an accident.

Boiler

The large open vat in which the pudding, or flesh, for hounds is boiled.

Bolt

Of horses: either to run away out of control or, if related to food, to gobble, leading only to indigestion. Of a fox: to force him out of a drain or earth with the aid of a terrier, stick or any other means.

Bone

The size and strength of a horse or hound is generally measured by his 'bone', that being the circumference of his leg immediately beneath the knee. An animal with 'plenty of bone' is considered strong and, if a horse, is therefore up to a lot of weight.

Bottom

Not what you are thinking, Sir! To a fox-hunter this means a big deep ditch. In some parts of the country a bottom is simply a very large ditch accompanied by a very large fence. In other parts it is first cousin to a ravine. It can also be called a dingle, ghyll, gill, dene or coombe.

Break, To

A fox breaks, or breaks covert, when he leaves a covert or woodland for the open.

Break out

A horse is said to break out when he sweats in the evening or at any other time of stress. Generally this has its origin in nervous causes.

Break up

A Kennelman breaks up the pudding, and mixes it with broth, before it is fed to the pack.

A pack of hounds break up a fox at the end of a successful hunt.

Breast plate

Forget Boadicea! This is an article of equine apparel designed to fit round the shoulders to prevent the saddle slipping back when going up steep places. People say it is unnecessary, but I would not like to have a day's stag-hunting or ride in very steep places on a horse with narrow shoulders without one. It is nearly always used by show jumpers and eventers.

Brow band

Part of the bridle, fitting round the front and top of the face, just below and in front of the ears. A controversial subject, as for hunting it should be made of plain, brown leather, and never be coloured. Coloured browbands are used for showing, so they can often be used by quite respectable people. My family are entitled to wear blue and buff browbands, for instance! However a coloured browband may often be accompanied by a made-up tie!

Brush

Of course you all know that this is a fox's tail. A horse is said to brush when he knocks the fetlock joint of one leg against the opposite joint of the other leg.

Brushing-boots

Brushing-boots are worn by horses, not to prevent brushing, but to prevent sore fetlock joints caused by brushing.

Bullfinch

A hedge so high that you cannot jump it, but not so thick that you cannot jump through it.

Bye-day
A day's hunting put in that does not appear in the list of appointments.

Cantle
The back of the saddle.

Cap, To
To collect money from someone who is out as a visitor and who does not subscribe to the Hunt.

Cast
A Huntsman makes his cast when hounds have lost the scent and failed to find it by themselves. He casts the pack first in the direction in which he thinks the fox has gone. The expression is also used when a horse has come down in its stable or horse-box, or has been thrown down for an operation.

Charlie
A name given, almost with affection, to foxes; deriving from Charles James Fox, the eighteenth-century politician.

Check
Hounds check, or stop, when they are unable to own the line – in other words when they lose the scent.
   A check is the time when hounds are checked, and sometimes provides a welcome breathing space.

Chopped
A fox is said to have been chopped if he is killed before he has a chance to run.

Country
The area hunted by a particular pack of hounds. They may only draw for a fox in their own country, but may run into another to catch it.

Couple
Two hounds.

Couples
Two collars that are so joined that hounds are linked together.

Coverts
Woods or coppices that are either natural or artificial and of any size, where a fox is likely to be found. They are fenced to stop stock from straying into them.

Crown in
Fill in a trench, as you dig on further.

Cry
The sound hounds make when running.

Cub-hunting
Sometimes loosely termed 'cubbing', an expression I personally deplore. These are early morning hunts that take place before the regular season starts, and they are designed to teach young hounds to hunt and cubs to run.

Curb
A bony enlargement protruding from the back of a horse's hock. It is a source of lameness, and so a technical unsoundness. It occurs more frequently in young horses that have done too much work.

Curb-bit
A bit that is used with a bridoon in a double bridle.

Curb-chain
This is used under the horse's chin with a curb-bit and with a Pelham. There should also be a chin-strap to prevent rubbing.

Cur-dog
Any dog other than a hound. Even the champion at Crufts would be so-called if it made an appearance in the hunting field.

Cut and laid, A
This is a hedge cut hard back; the top cut off, or some of it, and laced sideways along the top of the hedge. Alas, this is a dying art and not seen in many parts of the country.

Den
A term used in the USA and certain parts of the British Isles for a fox's earth. 'Denned' means 'gone to ground'.

Dock
The bony part of a horse's tail. To dock a terrier is to cut its tail, leaving just enough for it to be pulled out of holes.

Done
An exhausted horse, or one whose grooming has been finished.

Doubling
Sounding a series of double notes on a hunting horn.

Draft
To send hounds to another pack.

Drag
No, *not* a man riding side-saddle, but the scent left by a fox or other animal while on its nocturnal wanderings. Hounds 'drag' up to their quarry when they work out this stale line until they fresh-find him. A drag hunt is quite a different affair; a rag soaked in aniseed or fox's litter is literally dragged along to lay a scent for hounds to hunt.

Draw, To
Looking for a fox with hounds. To draw a hound is to separate one hound from the rest of the pack.

Earth
A fox's burrow, or den.

Enter
To enter a hound is to start it on its hunting career. To enter a terrier is to teach it to go to ground.

Feather, To
When hounds take a sudden and much more active interest they are said to feather. They move more quickly and their noses seem to be glued to the ground, their sterns moving furiously from side to side. With any luck, immediately afterwards you may expect to see the pack sweep away on the line.

Field, The
Mounted followers of a Hunt.

Foiled
Land which has acquired a strong unnatural smell, possibly because cattle or sheep have just gone across it, or because it has recently had artificial manure spread on it.

Give tongue, To
Quite simply, this is the noise made by hounds when they are hunting. It is utterly incorrect to call it barking!

Going
The nature of the ground as it affects a horse's ability to gallop, ie hard, heavy or deep, but unfortunately very seldom good!

Good head
When hounds are running well together with a broad front.

Graft
A crescent-bladed spade.

Green
A horse that is not fully trained or experienced – not to be recommended for your hunt staff (nor for you!)

Hand
Four inches; the accepted measurement of the palm of a hand. A horse is measured from the withers to the ground by means of a stick with a movable bar set at right angles, this being placed on the withers.

Hands, Good
A gift by which horsemen, by lightness of touch and some indefinable means, convey to their horse their every wish.

Head
To head a fox is to divert him from his original course. Do NOT do this near me.

Headland
The side of a field near the fence.

Heel
When hounds run a line the opposite way to that which the fox was going.

Hold up
To hold up a covert is to surround it so that cubs cannot get away during the cub-hunting season. It is also an expression used as a sharp reminder to a horse that has stumbled.

Holloa
A scream to denote that a fox has been sighted.

Holt
An otter's stronghold or den, generally under an old tree-trunk beside a river, with at least one entrance or exit under water.

Huick Holloa
Pronounced 'hike holler', means listen, or 'Hark, there's a holloa'.

Jink
To make a sudden sharp turn.

Kennel
The above-ground bed of a fox, so to un-kennel the fox is to make him leave it.

Kennel-huntsman
A man employed not only to look after the hounds, but also to hunt them.

Lark

We have to get up with it in the cub-hunting season, as scent is better in the early morning at that time of year. It is also an expression used to describe the actions of foolish people who jump fences unnecessarily and at the wrong time.

Leash

A leash of foxes is three foxes on foot.

Lift

A Huntsman 'lifts' hounds when he has reason to believe that the fox has gone much further ahead, and that by doing so they will be enabled to hit off the line again.

Livery

A hunt servant's uniform. When payment is made for the feeding and stabling of a horse it is said to be at 'livery'.

Made

A horse is said to be 'made' when not only has he been broken in, but also been ridden to hounds or hacked until he is possessed of good manners.

Mark

When hounds bay outside an earth, the fox having gone to ground.

Mask

The fox's head (either dead or alive).

MFHA

The Masters of Foxhounds Association – a governing body that devotes itself to the well-being of the Hunts that are its members, this membership carrying many privileges.

Music

The finest sound to my mind that there can be – the noise that hounds make when they are running.

Mute

Hounds running without giving tongue – a very serious fault.

Nappy

This describes a horse that may put in a sudden buck or fly-jump, or refuse to move. It covers a multitude of sins.

Nerve

The opposite of nerves.

Nose

A sense of smell when relating to a hound. A hound with a good nose will therefore have good smelling power, and be able to make use of it in terms of action.

Open

The first hound to speak.

Over at the knees

Knees bent too far forward. There are two sorts, the natural and the acquired. The natural are those with which a horse is foaled, and the acquired are the result of very hard work. Legs that stand over naturally never fail and are not considered a fault, but those acquired have failed already.

Over-ride

To ride too close to the hounds, which does not give them enough freedom to hunt properly.

Overshot

When a hound's upper jaw protrudes in front of his lower jaw – the opposite of swine-chopped.

Own the line

Pick up the scent again that has been lost.

Pad

A fox's foot, which is sometimes given to followers as a trophy.

Pipe opener

A gallop to clear a horse's wind, rather as an athlete limbers up before a race.

Poached

Ground that has been broken up by the hooves of stock.

Point

The point of a hunt is the distance between the two farthest-apart points of the hunt as the crow flies. It is an expression often used to describe the distance between the find and the finish of a hunt, again as the crow flies, and not as hounds run.

Provinces

All hunting countries of England, Scotland and Wales, except the Shire Countries which are the Pytchley, the Quorn, the Fernie, the Cottesmore and the Belvoir.

Proving the line

Casting hounds and re-casting until the line the fox has taken is hit off.

Pye
A foxhound colour that is lighter than tan; varieties are lemon, hare and badger.

Rate
To correct a hound – a function for hunt staff only.

Ribbon
A red ribbon should be put up in a horse's tail if you know he is likely to kick. If your horse is young and uncertain, a green ribbon should be used. Should you find your horse is being difficult when you are out, put one hand behind your back when going through narrow places as this will act as a warning to others following.

Ride
A wide path through a covert – generally man-made.

Ringing
A ringing fox is one that runs in circles, never going very far from where it is found.

Riot
When hounds hunt anything that moves, apart from what they should be hunting.

Roach-back
A back which makes an upward curve, or a horse which deliberately arches his back when his rider mounts.

Roots
Root crops such as turnips, swedes, beets, mangolds, potatoes etc.

Roughed off
A horse that is being 'let down' at the end of the season, by being turned out in a field by day and given lower rations in preparation for being turned out altogether.

Scarlet
This is the more generally accepted term for a red coat, though people do persist in using the expression 'pink'. The use of 'red coat' is also acceptable.

Sett
The stronghold of a badger.

Shelly
A hound is said to be shelly when he is weak and wasp-waisted.

Sinking
A fox is said to be sinking when he is running out of strength and weakening.

Skipping
Picking up odd droppings in the stable.

Skirt, To
When a hound cuts corners and doesn't work out the true line of a fox.

Snipey head
One that tends to be narrow and pointed in a hound.

Soil
If a stag stands at bay in a pond or river he is said to have soiled. He also soils when he rolls in a pool of water, which he does regularly.

Speak
Hounds speak, or give tongue. A thrilling moment.

Stake and bound, A
Upright stakes bound horizontally.

Stale
An expression used for equine and hound urination. It also means a horse that has been over-trained and has become so bored that he is lethargic and unwilling.

Stale line
The line of a fox that was there a long time ago, and the scent is therefore almost non-existent. Very rarely your hunted fox.

Stallion-hound
A male hound used for breeding purposes.

Star gazer
A horse that carries his head too high and therefore takes his fences blindly.

Staring coat
A dull coat in both horse and hound. One in which the hairs do not lie flat and denote general malaise.

Stern, A
A hound's tail.

Sticky
A horse that half refuses at a jump, and then takes it from a standstill – a very uncomfortable ride.

Sticky going
When you, and you hope your horse, must look where you are going.

Stoutness
Strength both in looks and in general well-being.

Strapper
A person employed to work in stables under the supervision of the Stud-groom, who is in charge.

Swine-chopped
When a hound's lower jaw protrudes beyond his upper jaw.

Tack
Terrible modern-day jargon for what should be Saddlery. Stable requisites, but when correctly used means grooming kit.

Tail hounds
Hounds which are somewhat behind the main body of the pack.

Tally ho!
A hunting cry that means 'I have seen a fox'.

Tally over!
A hunting cry that means 'I have seen a fox cross the ride'.

Teeth
Two middle 'nippers' you behold
Before the colt is two weeks old.
Before eight weeks two more will come,
Eight months the 'corners' cut the gum.
A horse is said to have a full mouth when it is six years old.

Throw up
When hounds cannot own a line.

Thruster
One who pushes his way regardless of other people.

Timber
Post and rails, or hunt jumps made of wood.

Tops
An expression used to describe the band of lighter-coloured leather at the top of hunting-boots.

Trencher-fed
A trencher-fed pack means that individual hounds or maybe a couple or two are kept by farmers, at home. They are brought to the Meet on a hunting day, and then taken home again in the evening.

Tubed horse
One that has gone in the wind, and has had a tube inserted in his windpipe to assist breathing. Don't swim a river on one of these.

Twitch
A device consisting of a piece of wood with a hole in it through which is threaded a piece of cord. This is put round the upper lip of the horse, and then the wood is twisted, and the horse's mind one hopes is therefore taken away from other nasty things that may be happening to it.

Tyro
A beginner.

Un-entered hounds
Hounds that have not yet been introduced to their quarry.

Valeting room
Where hunt servants clean their clothes.

View
To see a fox is to 'view' it.

Voluntary
A fall. Another expression is 'to own' a piece of land.

Walk
To walk a hound puppy is to bring him up in your own home after he has been weaned.

Walking out
Hound exercise – in other words, disciplined walks.

Whelps
Unweaned puppies.

Wind
For a hound the act of smelling a fox is known as 'winding' the fox. When used for a horse, it refers to the respiratory processes, eg 'gone in the wind'.

Wolf's tooth
A second tooth that does not grow immediately under a temporary middle tooth but by its side, so that the permanent tooth is pushed out of place. It tends to cut the cheek, prevents proper grinding of corn and can cause all manner of trouble.

Woodland
A very large covert, that to anyone but a fox-hunter would just be called a wood or a forest.

Bibliography

Baily's Hunting Directory (J. A. Allen).

Barton, F. T., MRCVS. *Horses and Practical Horse-Keeping* (Jarrold & Sons, 1910).

Beaufort, Duke of and Morris, Mowbray. *Hunting*, in the Badminton Library (Longmans, Green & Co, 1885).

Beckford, Peter. *Thoughts on Hunting* (Methuen & Sons Ltd, 1779).

Bell, Isaac, MFH. *Foxiana* (Country Life, 1929).

Bloodgood, Lida Fleitmann and Piero Santini. *The Horseman's Dictionary* (Pelham Books, 1963).

Brander, Michael. *Hunting and Shooting* (Weidenfeld & Nicolson, 1971).

Brock, D. W. E., MFH. *Stablecraft* (H. F. & G. Witherby Ltd, 1937).
——. *The Foxhunter's Week-end Book* (Seeley Service & Co Ltd, 1939).

Bromley Davenport, W. *Sport* (Chapman & Hall, 1888).

Brooke, Lt. Col. Geoffrey, DSO, MC. *Horse-sense and Horsemanship of Today* (Constable & Co Ltd, 1924).

Brown, Thomas, MPS. *A Manual of Modern Farriery* (James S. Virtue, mid-nineteenth century).

Brusewitz, Gunnar. *Hunting* (George Allen & Unwin Ltd, 1969).

Burrows, Roger. *Wild Fox* (David & Charles, 1969: Pan Books, 1973).

Campbell, Barry. *The Badminton Tradition* (Michael Joseph, 1971).

Carr, Raymond. *English Fox Hunting* (Weidenfeld & Nicolson, 1976).

Clapham, Richard. *The Book of the Fox* (Herbert Jenkins Ltd, 1936).

Clayton, Michael. *A Hunting We Will Go* (J. A. Allen & Co, 1967).

Cox, Nicholas. *The Gentleman's Recreation (Hunting)* (J. C., 1677).

Dale, T. E. *The Eighth Duke of Beaufort and the Badminton Hunt* (Archibald Constable & Co Ltd, 1901).

Davies, E. W. L. *Memoir of the Rev. John Russell of Tordown* (Richard Bentley & Son, 1883).

Delabere, Blaine. *Canine Pathology* (Longman, Orme & Co, 1841).

Egerton Warburton, R. E. *Hunting Songs* (Pickering & Co, 1883).

Fawcett, William. *The Sportman's Library Fox-Hunting* (Philip Allan, 1936).

Fisher, Major Arthur. *Through Stable and Saddle Room* (Richard Bentley & Son, 1891).

Foxford, *Horse and Hound Foxhunting Companion* (Country Life Books, 1978).

Goldschmidt, Lt. Col. Sidney G. *An Eye for a Horse* (Constable & Co Ltd, 1932).

Gordon Mackenzie, Captain Courtlandt, R A. *Notes for Hunting Men* (Longmans, Green & Co, 1901).

Hayes, Captain Horace M., FRCVS. *Riding and Hunting* (Hurst & Blackett Ltd, 1910).

James, David and Stephens, Wilson (Eds). *In Praise of Hunting* (Hollis & Carter, 1960).

Kerr, Eleanor. *Hunting Parson* (Herbert Jenkins, 1963).

Ligertwood, Kenneth. *Huntsmen of Our Time* (Pelham Books, 1968).

Lindley Wood, E. *Smooth Fox Terriers* (W. & G. Foyle Ltd, 1960).

Lommel, Andreas. *The World of the Early Hunters* (Evelyn, Adams & Mackay, 1967).

Lonsdale, Earl of (Ed). *Foxhunting,* in the Lonsdale Library (Seeley Service & Co, 1930).

Lonsdale, Earl of and Parker, Eric. *Horsemanship,* in the Lonsdale Library (Seeley Service & Co Ltd, 1948).

Lucas, Sir Jocelyn. *Hunt and Working Terriers* (Chapman & Hall, 1931).

Lutyens, F. M. *Mr Spinks and His Hounds* (Vinton & Co, 1890).

Mery, Fernard. *The Dog* (Cassell, 1968).

Mills, John. *The Life of a Foxhound* (Philip Allan, 1848).

Moore, Daphne. *Famous Foxhunters* (Spur Publications, 1978).

Nimrod, 'The Chace'. *The Quarterly Review* (1832).

Richardson, Charles. *Practical Hints for Hunting Novices* (Horace Cox, 1906).

Russell, Dan. *Working Terriers, Their Training and Management in the Field* (The Batchworth Press, 1948).

Scott, Walter. *Guy Mannering* (1829).

Serrell, Alys F. *With Hound and Terrier in the Field* (Edited by Frances Slaughter) (William Blackwood & Sons, 1904).

Sheddon, Lady Diana and Apsley, Lady. *To Whom the Goddess* (Hutchinson & Co, 1932).

Somerville, E. OE. (Collector). *Notes of the Horn* (Peter Davies, 1934).

Sparrow, Geoffrey, MC, TD, FRCS. *The Terrier's Vocation* (J. A. Allen & Co, 1949).

Summerhays, R. S. *Elements of Hunting* (Country Life, 1938).

Surtees, R. S. *Jorrocks* (George Routledge & Sons Ltd, mid-nineteenth century).

Vesey-Fitzgerald, Brian. *Town Fox, Country Fox* (André Deutsch, 1965: Corgi, 1973).

Wentworth Day, J. *The Dog in Sport* (George G. Harrap & Co Ltd, 1938).

Whyte Melville, G. J. *Riding Recollections* (Country Life, 1933).

Willoughby, the Hon. Charles. *The Sporting Scene, Come and Hunt* (Museum Press, 1952).

Willoughby de Broke, Lord. *Hunting the Fox* (Constable & Co Ltd, 1925).

Index